The Young Adult's Guide to

Surviving Dorm Life

Skills & Strategies for Handling Roommates

WITHDRAWN

By Melanie Falconer

THE YOUNG ADULT'S GUIDE TO SURVIVING DORM LIFE: SKILLS & STRATEGIES FOR HANDLING ROOMMATES

1405 SW 6th Avenue • Ocala, Florida 34471 • Phone 800-814-1132 • Fax 352-622-1875
Website: www.atlantic-pub.com • Email: sales@atlantic-pub.com
SAN Number: 268-1250

Library of Congress Cataloging-in-Publication Data

Names: Falconer, Melanie, author.
Title: The young adult's guide to surviving dorm life : skills & strategies for handling roommates / Melanie Falconer.
Description: Ocala, Florida : Atlantic Publishing Group, Inc., [2017] | Includes bibliographical references and index.
Identifiers: LCCN 2017004465 (print) | LCCN 2017016004 (ebook) | ISBN 9781620232026 (ebook) | ISBN 9781620232019 (alk. paper) | ISBN 1620232014 (alk. paper)
Subjects: LCSH: Dormitory life. | Roommates. | College student orientation.
Classification: LCC LB3227 (ebook) | LCC LB3227 .F35 2017 (print) | DDC 378.1/9871--dc23
LC record available at https://lccn.loc.gov/2017004465

Printed in the United States

PROJECT MANAGER AND EDITOR: Rebekah Sack
ASSISTANT EDITOR: Rebekah Slonim
INTERIOR LAYOUT AND JACKET DESIGN: Nicole Sturk • nicolejonessturk@gmail.com

Reduce. Reuse.
RECYCLE.

A decade ago, Atlantic Publishing signed the Green Press Initiative. These guidelines promote environmentally friendly practices, such as using recycled stock and vegetable-based inks, avoiding waste, choosing energy-efficient resources, and promoting a no-pulping policy. We now use 100-percent recycled stock on all our books. The results: in one year, switching to post-consumer recycled stock saved 24 mature trees, 5,000 gallons of water, the equivalent of the total energy used for one home in a year, and the equivalent of the greenhouse gases from one car driven for a year.

Over the years, we have adopted a number of dogs from rescues and shelters. First there was Bear and after he passed, Ginger and Scout. Now, we have Kira, another rescue. They have brought immense joy and love not just into our lives, but into the lives of all who met them.

We want you to know a portion of the profits of this book will be donated in Bear, Ginger and Scout's memory to local animal shelters, parks, conservation organizations, and other individuals and nonprofit organizations in need of assistance.

— Douglas & Sherri Brown,
President & Vice-President of Atlantic Publishing

Table of Contents

Introduction

The first few days of living with my roommate were unbelievably shocking and uncomfortable.

To provide a little context, I was a single child who grew up with a single mother who was out of the house working once I was a teenager. It was an absolute fantasy, complete with all the privacy and freedom any adolescent desires. The house was my playground for hours on end, a site for my hidden persona as a rock-star virtuoso and a safe space for my new dance moves.

As they say, all good things must come to an end. Dare I say, once I started living with a roommate in a college dorm, the good things crashed and burned.

My roommate grew up in Southern California, which might as well be located in a different galaxy than my home in the small liberal mecca that is the Bay Area. She liked dubstep. I liked folk music from the '60s. She was compulsively clean and compared my side of the room to "an old New York ghetto before the city implemented hygiene standards." She watched reality television, countless YouTube videos, music videos, new webisodes from new web series, and I watched nothing, ever. I read, or tried to, while her iPhone speakers blasted for hours.

We fought. We had at least several major blowouts that resulted in outside intervention. Both of us seriously contemplated finding other roommates.

The funny thing about humans, though, is we share things in common. There are things that connect us no matter how different we perceive others to be. We like to be respected. We want to trust. We need to be good communicators in order to get what we need and deserve. Fortunately enough for her and me, we had skilled residential advisors who helped us work through our issues. We established ground rules, effective ways of communicating with each other, and could then create relative harmony until the following year when we picked new roommates to live with.

Did she and I become *the best of friends?* No. The single most important thing above becoming buddies when you live together is *learning how to live together.* It's not learning how to sing together, cook together, or frolic in a field together; it's learning how you two can cohabitate without seething every time your roommate walks in the door. Perhaps you were lucky enough to learn these skills growing up with a sibling, but maybe you weren't. Either way, chances are, you will have to learn these in college and beyond into young adulthood, where high rents may force you into a small space with another living, breathing, mess-making human being.

Don't be discouraged. This book is going to teach you the skills necessary to understand, learn, and prepare for the inevitable — if you pay attention.

Chapter 1

Dipping Your Feet In: The Dorms, a New Home, and a New Roommate

Before Your Arrival

Take a look at your hometown. There are things you will miss and things you will not. Maybe there's a man who gets just a little too happy to play an acoustic guitar at one o'clock in the morning on your street corner. You don't need to say goodbye to him: just smile and wave. There are certainly coffee shops, parks, restaurants, theaters, or monuments that have given your city or town a certain charm that will always remind you of your days growing up. Whether you do this alone or with a friend, make plans to visit each of these places. Make it a sort of ceremony, a way to make peace with your past and move on to your future.

Whether you're moving just a town over or a couple of states over, this is time you need to make for yourself to register the fact that you're an adult now. Mom and Dad won't be driving you to soccer practice: you'll be walking there or finding a way to get there yourself. Brace yourself for the many peanut butter and jelly sandwiches that you will eat as you try to teach yourself how to cook or the many meals you will consume at the dining hall.

And, most important: you will be living with someone your age, at your maturity level, in a dorm room.

Maybe you've received a housing questionnaire and roommate preference forms in the mail. Maybe you tend to kick stale pizza crusts under your bed but selected the "I prefer a neat roommate" checkbox. Perhaps you like to study from midnight to 3 a.m., but noted you are an "early riser."

These questionnaires will not be graded. There are no right or wrong answers, so therefore you shouldn't feel like you have to present yourself as someone you're not. Your answer *will* affect how your first year of college will inevitably play out, which is why campus housing professionals will say that the first rule in filling out these forms is to be honest.

If you are allergic to cigarette smoke, do not indicate that you do not mind living with a smoker. If you tend to be on the shy side and it takes a while before you open up, do not paint yourself as someone who loves socializing. This is also not the time to experiment with reverse psychology. Indicating that you are a neat freak in your preferences when you are not does not mean you will get assigned to a neat freak that will do all the cleaning. Also, do not assume that if you are matched with an honor student that he or she will help you study. The exact opposite will happen. This person will resent your laziness, lack of enthusiasm, and will wonder what he or she did to deserve a living situation comparable to "The Odd Couple."[1]

Moving into a residence hall and starting college is a huge step into adulthood. It can be overwhelming, especially if you have never lived away from home. If your inclination is to run back to Mom and Dad after the second day (especially if the first impression of your roommate is less than stellar), give it at least a few weeks. If you look back wishing that you had been more honest on the questionnaires, learn from it, and move on.

Introduce yourself to the other people living in your dorms. Have a conversation, get to know each other, and then be prepared for them to get on your last nerve and for them to tell you the same. It is just like living with your family, but with different rules and unlimited internet access. But just like living with family, know there will be good times too: look at the events calendar, check out things around town, and go out with your dorm-mates to lunch or dinner. Soon enough, you'll feel right at home.

---

1. "The Odd Couple" is a play by Neil Simon about an incredibly slobby sports journalist who lets his recently divorced and obsessively clean friend come stay with him.

Meanwhile, Back at the Dorm . . .

Did you know that some colleges have specific themes for certain dorm complexes? It's similar to Harry Potter, if you want to think about it that way. When reading up about the different dorms, pay careful attention to the culture of each and every one. One might be intended for students who share an interest in creative arts, another for those who are more bookish, and another toward more technologically-inclined students. Make sure to look up student reviews online before selecting which one you'll inevitably live in; it can mean the difference between feeling a part of a community and feeling completely isolated. ■

A Word for the Wise . . .

Conflict is an essential part of life. In fact, it's the only thing that makes you grow. Accept that you may have a roommate who you disagree with, but take it as an opportunity to mature and learn for next time.

Considerations and Tips for Off-Campus Housing

There are some colleges that will require you to live in the dorms for a certain portion of your time in college. They might require one or two years of dorm living before they allow you to live off campus. Some financial obligations or other situations may require that you live off campus instead. If you need to spend the first couple of years of college living off campus, we recommend that you don't live with your parents. Find a place with other people your age instead. Here are a few compelling reasons why:

- **You're becoming an adult.** In order for you to grow up you'll need to move out. It will become too easy to lean on your parents for things you should be doing yourself. Do you really want to come back from your

"Semantics of Reason" class to find your mother folding your laundry? At the same time, your parents will most likely treat you like they always have. Now is the time to live without limitations and experiment to find out how you want to live. Unless you want to have to call your parents when you want to stay out late at a party, then be our guest.

- **You'll miss out.** Where the dorms basically force students to be social, you will have to go out of your way to make friends. Not saying this is difficult, as you can find plenty of clubs and study groups to join, but you'll miss out on all those small but crucial casual lunches with dorm-mates and spontaneous study sessions with your roommate. Ideally, if you live off campus, you'll find other people your age (and in your situation) that go to the same school so you don't miss out on making meaningful friendships.

- **You might be isolating yourself from the university community.** Unless you find a place super close to the university, you might be unknowingly isolating yourself from your school's community. A lot of the time, the dorm's "provost," a community leader of sorts, will bring in lecturers to come speak to the students in the dorms, plan big potlucks for the residents, and arrange field trips where everyone can bond together. Even if you find an apartment with students who go to the school, you could be unintentionally isolating yourself from a whole other vibrant community within the university.

- **Living with housemates is a good way to see what life after college will be like.** That's right, living with housemates in a shared housing or apartment situation will most likely be your situation once you graduate. In fact, it may be a good thing for you to test out during college, instead of being shocked once you start apartment hunting in the real world!

To Bring or Not to Bring?

No matter where you're moving to, be it in a cozy room in the dorms or a new apartment, you have to decide what you're going to bring. Chances are it won't even be half of what you own. As a matter of fact, our first recommendation is that it's *less* than half.

Just like packing for a trip, when you bring something you feel you "simply cannot live without for five days," remember that just about anything you will need at college you will be able to find or buy, Unless you are studying abroad, or have special medical needs that require a prescription, even the most remote private colleges will have resources and access to items you may need but did not bring from home. Keep in mind the space will seem much smaller once you, and possibly one or two other roommates, unpack and get settled.

Here's a list of the common items you'll find in most residence halls that you most likely won't needy to worry about packing:

- A single bed

- A desk

- Mirrors

- Carpet

- Appliances such as refrigerator and microwave

- Closets

- Ethernet connections

- Televisions in the community rooms

Most universities post an online checklist of "things to bring" or a list of items to coordinate with your roommate, such as coffeemaker, stereo, and other small furniture items. Pay close attention to this list if your university provides it, because some items may never occur to you, such as umbrella, first-aid items, basic tools, and hangers. If your university does not provide a "what to bring list," it should provide you with a list of things *not* to bring, such as halogen lamps, candles, incense, weapons, pets (some universities allow fish!), or open-coil cooking appliances.

A Word for the Wise . . .

I brought a coffeemaker with me at the beginning of my second year. I went out to the dollar store downtown and bought a dollar tin of coffee and some paper cups, and then sold 10 cups of coffee per pot to the unprepared, caffeine-starved students in my residence hall. On a good night, usually during exam weeks, I could make $30.

Just remember: you don't want to be the bug-eyed, over-eager scout falling over with your overloaded backpack, but you definitely don't want to be braving the wild with just you and a can opener. Bring what's necessary to plant and fertilize the seed, and let the other things (posters, decorations, furniture) follow organically from establishing the basics.

First Assignment: Explore Your Surroundings

Scan your new environment like a hawk. Maybe all you want to do is go about the usual: play on your laptop, scroll infinitely through your social media feed, check your email, wrap up in some blankets, watch Netflix and then zonk out. That's what I did for a bit. Was I blissfully content for a couple of hours? Yes. Were these the habits that ended up helping me establishing lifelong friendships and connections that would continue to bring me happiness even *after* college? Did they help me have some real adventures and see some new things? No and no.

Think of college and living in the dorms (or off-campus apartment) as a vacation from real life, your parents, and your annoying little sisters. Let's go over some must-sees during your grand tour.

The academy or community of residence halls

Remember how we talked about the community your dorm hall resides in? Sometimes they're referred to fancifully as "academies" or on much simpler terms as a "dorm community" or as different "colleges" within your university. They will most likely share a common student culture. Some might lean more towards fitness and health, complete with a beautiful gym and a natural grocery mart just steps away from the dorms. Others might lean towards different interests or philosophies, one community hosting more international students, the other appealing to liberal arts–minded students with a large library, book clubs, and art galleries. The list goes on and on.

The best way to know what's going on is to look at the events board. We challenge you to make the effort to go to at least one of the listed events within your first three weeks.

The campus

You've probably taken the tour, but now that it's official, you'll want to take an in-depth look at the campus. First, make sure to walk around to all the major coffee shops, libraries, and lounges and make a list of your five favorite ones. Then, take note of all the quick marts, bus routes, the location of the financial aid office, student health center, the various academic departments, campus security office, and the main library. Oh, and don't forget your class schedule with the building and room numbers so you know exactly where you need to go during your first week!

The new town or city

If your college is practically in your parents' backyard, this won't apply to you, but maybe you're in a *completely different city than the one you left.* This is, undoubtedly, scary and exciting. The best part is that you'll be making so many new friends to experience the city with. If you want to build up some major cred, make sure to go out and explore on the weekends. Find out the best bike paths, restaurants, town relics, and all the nooks and crannies that make a city or town special.

Better yet, find *your* personal getaway spots where you can distance yourself from the stress of school — or a potentially stressful living situation.

Second Assignment: Scope Out the Dorms

When it comes to first starting out in the dorms, here are a couple of strategies to make your time with your peers as sane, comfortable, and drama-free as the circumstances will permit. Unless you want your experience to be like an episode out of MTV's "Real World," here is a quick set of recommendations for you to follow:

Don't be an open book

You'd be surprised at the kind of people you'll meet during your freshman year. Most problems come from when students still have fresh, unresolved issues and don't seek out help for them. People can become stalkers or unhealthily obsessive over a person. Some students may feel desperate for friendship, but end up becoming a pest who doesn't know his or her boundaries yet. Even if you're an extrovert, it's best to play shy, get a feel for everyone, and then get to know everyone at a steady pace to avoid unwanted situations — unless you want to awkwardly pass by someone you're trying to unfriend when you wake up in the morning every day.

Keep your doors open the first couple of days

If you have a hard time being direct, this is a great way to send the signal that you're open to meeting new people. If you bring a coffeemaker you can get to know people over a nice cup of joe right there in your dorm.

Get close, but not too close

Of course, if you meet the Patrick to your SpongeBob, the peanut butter to your jelly, go for it. But don't lean on relationships in your dorms too much because, if you think about it, they're a little artificial and based on familiarity. Two mice in a cage will eventually end up friends, right? While this may come off as a little harsh, remember that the friendships that last you a lifetime are based on core values, shared interests and viewpoints. You should always be cordial to your dorm-mates, but make sure to take initiative in your classes and forge friendships with people interested in the same things — these are the ones that will usually last.

A Word for the Wise . . .

Out of all my dorm-mates in college, I'm only friends with one. Graduating college was not too long ago for me, either. He is a great conversationalist, loves interesting ideas, and has a sarcastic but goofy sense of humor like I do. When I lived in the dorms though, I felt intensely close with everyone! It was only after living an adult life and getting a better sense of myself that I realized it was only really because we were in constant contact.

Third Assignment: Meeting Your College Roommate

Living with a college roommate can be a rewarding and enriching experience. For your roommate experience to be a success, you will have to cooperate. Sharing a room with someone is like a relationship or marriage: there has to be compromise and flexibility for it to work. You will have to accept another person and all his or her faults in order to stay sane. And of course, you have the benefit of moving on to another living arrangement without filing for a divorce.

In addition to new educational experiences, the experience of sharing a small space with other students is an education in itself. Your roommate may come from a different cultural, religious, or economic background. He or she may have grown up on a farm in Iowa, whereas you may have lived in a New York high-rise. He or she may be Jewish; you may be a devout Catholic. His or her family may be involved in every major decision he makes, while yours is letting you find your way.

Despite these differences and the potential for conflict, don't worry. Just remember, you are sharing the new college and new roommate experience with thousands of other 18-year olds around the country and the world. As long as you keep your head on straight, the reality television producers won't be cold-calling you to audition for their new special: "The New Crazy: Living in College Dorms."

The best advice we have for meeting your new roommate is to share, but keep your personality to yourself. You may decide that you don't like your roommate very much for whatever reason. Maybe he or she orders pizza way too often, and you think the smell is disgusting. Maybe they don't take out the boxes for a while (I certainly didn't). Whatever the reasons may be, keep them to yourself. If you come off as reserved at first, your roommate is far less likely to take it personally when you're not very talkative. This way, you can keep your focus outside of your room, and make friendships there.

If you do decide that you like your roommate, that's all the better. Frolic away!

Third or Fourth Roommate?

You may be shocked or surprised to hear that it's even possible to have a third or fourth roommate. In most cases, it's cheaper to share a room, though certainly more crowded. Sometimes a school's student body will be increasing at a rate that construction can't keep up with, so more people are crowded in tinier spaces.

In any cases, don't be discouraged if you end up having to share a space with two or more people. It can even have a neutralizing effect on the whole room dynamic. What do I mean by this? Well, if you don't like one of your roommates, then it's pretty easy to phase into the background and just smile, nod, and secretly seethe inside when they acknowledge you. Think of the other roommates as distractions, people you can redirect your energy toward instead of focusing on the negative.

In this situation, you also have a more expansive tribe. While the other people in the dorms are stuck being intensely dependent and close with just one other person, in this situation you have a rainbow of personalities and a wide support network. If one is out to class, the other might be available to have lunch with you. And hey, you brought a huge trunk of books? Your roommates are built-in movers and can help you lug that thing up the stairs!

Of course, many might see it as a nightmare. I mean, what if every single one of them has a partner? How in the world is that supposed to work? Maybe it's finals week, and all you want is a little alone time. Maybe you're feeling blue and need your own private box to hole up in, a way for you to just say "NO" to the entire world. Unfortunately, privacy is, in fact, a luxury. Maybe one day someone will think to put it in the Constitution, but for now, it's a pricy commodity. It's better to think of this as an opportunity to expand your circle and perhaps even avoid the intense conflict that tends to arise in pairs, rather than groups of three or four.

Meanwhile, Back at the Dorm . . .

So, what if you don't like your roommate? Roommates, even?

You might find yourself spending a little too much time in the community dorm lounge than you care to, feeling like that awkward coffee shop regular that realizes they know the baristas and customers just a little too well. You start talking it up with other dorm-mates who are probably there because they also have a roommate who leaves a trail of garbage behind them. Maybe you find a flowery field to frolic in to celebrate your newfound friendship! What a beautiful thing! Right?

Yes and no. The problem is, your roommate(s) could get jealous if they see you making an effort with other dorm-mates and not with them, feel rejected, or irritated by you fleeing constantly from them. Avoiding them may end up making things even worse because they'll see you trying to make yourself invisible and guess what? They'll treat you like you're invisible. Or, they might get resentful and confront you in passive-aggressive ways. Even if they're not your favorite people, make a commitment to do one thing with them a week just to maintain a common ground with them. Study session, dinner, movie, grocery shopping, midnight walk, whatever.

This way, you can continue to get to know other people in the dorm, while knowing things back in your room are cool and collected. ∎

You May Be Best Friends Now

Your best friend—you have known each other since second grade and spent more time at each other's homes the past few years than your own. Half of the clothes in your closet belong to her. That is obviously fabulous. Lifelong friendships can be more rewarding and successful than those with your family. But it does not make for a successful relationship as college roommates. Many colleges strongly recommended that you not live with a close friend and may even state this in housing literature.

If you can't think of why that could be, consider: one of you gets a boyfriend before the other. He is there often. Your best friend has less time for you and is hanging the "Come back later, I'm studying" note on the door more often. Here is another: One of you joins a sorority and the other does not. Now you have moved into new realm of social relationships and your soon-to-be-ex-best friend is jealous.

A Word for the Wise . . .

You might be tempted to say, "Well, she's so different from me that we can learn from each other!" While this may be true, consider my own account: I had a friend who, during high school, was incredibly successful. I remained in my corner of the cafeteria reading comic books, dreaming when I should've been studying. Once college came around, the tables had turned: I ended up acing all my college classes from the very beginning. She came close to failing.

We thought of living together, until jealousy and resentment started tearing our friendship apart. It was only after some time and distance that we went back to being close friends.

If you must be near your best friend in college, live in the same hall, even on the same floor, but not in the same room. If you want to truly become best friends forever, the kind that give their kids names that rhyme (how about Alyssa and Clarissa?), and chill out in heaven taking some epic selfies with their new angel wings, have some foresight before deciding to live with him or her. Or, better yet, get caught up on some of the more sensational celebrity divorces. At one time, these people also thought they could not live without each other.

Reasons why rooming with a friend or best friend are not a good idea:

- One of you will get a girlfriend or boyfriend before the other. This may cause the friend to feel like an outsider and create jealousy.

- You are entering a new phase of your life and may outgrow the friendship.

- One of you is a social butterfly. The other isn't, doesn't make many friends, and gets jealous.

- One of you is busier and more motivated than the other, who would rather count the birds outside of their window while he or she plays Tetris.

- College is not high school. This is a different world. If you expect college to be an extension of high school, you are in for a big disappointment. In college, you'll be more stressed, and stress creates friction.

If you were insistent upon rooming with an old friend, and the agreement was mutual, it is likely one of you will move in a different direction, outgrow the friendship, or mature quicker than the other. This will lead to tension and confusion as your friend may be asking herself, "I don't get it. We used to be so close and now we hardly talk to each other any more." You are both experiencing new surroundings, relationships, and a higher level of expectations. All new students are going through a period of adjustment, so don't be too hard on yourself.

If you find yourself in that situation, here are a few strategies on how to approach your friend, and now roommate:

• If your old friend is clinging and looking to you to be her only friend and lifeboat as she treads new waters, be honest, but not hurtful with your feelings:

> "I know things are different now for both of us, but I want this to work. We just need a little space, you know, spend less time together and make new friends."

If she responds that your comments hurt her feelings, be gentle. Think about all the fun experiences you had together before college. You want to respect this friendship, but you want her to be realistic and respect your need to mature and grow.

• If the tension level is high and you are both asking yourselves why you ever thought living together would be a good idea, but do not want to abandon the situation, look at the glass as half full, rather than half empty:

> "I know things are tense right now, and we're both experiencing new things, but that doesn't mean we still can't live together."

Then, have a productive discussion on where the tension centers, what the conflicting issues are, and how you can both move forward and remain friends.

If you both get to a point where living together will destroy your friendship, and you both have acknowledged such, it may be time to split and move on to new roommates for the next semester. Hopefully, your friendship has not been permanently damaged, and it may even flourish and go the next level by living apart but staying in touch. After all, you have a bond that may go back to first grade, and that is rare in a society that has become more transient and fast-paced than ever. So hold onto him or her, but *don't* live with him or her.

CASE STUDY: OUR BEST FRIENDS MAY BE MONSTERS IN HIDING

Hannah Rose
Humboldt State University

Still not convinced? How a person acts when you're not around will never be accessible information around you. *Almost everyone* has monsters in their closet that they prefer to keep secret: the key is that some monsters are worse than others. We mainly keep these shadowy parts of ourselves reserved for when we're alone: i.e., at our home. Hence, your best friend could really be almost an entirely different person to live with and usually for the worst, not for the better.

Hannah Rose, a college student at Humboldt State, shares a rather horrific tale:

"When I first moved here, I was so excited to move in to my dorm and to be sharing it with my on-again-off-again best friend. About a month before we moved to Humboldt, we got this handy map of what our apartment looked like, and we were assigned sides of the room. Each side had a number that you were specifically given, and all of the furniture on that side would have that number engraved on it.

My roommate/best friend was lucky enough to get there an hour before me, and, when I arrived, she had moved in on *my side*. I was furious, but my parents calmed me down and told me I would not want to start my college experience off with an argument.

Fast forward to a few months later, when we got into a HUGE argument about how I go out of my way for her, she walks all over me, and how she doesn't respect me at all. I bring up the fact that she moved in on my side (thinking that at this point she may decide to apologize), but she almost proudly acknowledges that she did that on purpose because that side had more space and windows.

Later on in the year, I came home from an eight-and-a-half-hour shift at Taco Bell to find her and majority of the close friends I had made freshman year drinking in the room. Some were on my bed, one was in my chair, and I really wanted each and every one of them gone. I just wanted to be alone and relax. So I said hello, grabbed my PJs and books, and went to the living room to study.

Immediately after I left, they started gossiping about me. She went on and on about how awful I was to live with and that I was "such a toxic person to be around." All of my "friends" were agreeing, and after hearing them talk nonstop about me for five minutes, I walked back in there. She immediately started crying, realizing I had heard, and the other people started asking her if she was okay. I grabbed some of my stuff, and they begged me to stay. I told her not to touch any of my belongings, and I'd move out as soon as possible.

Many things had been leading up to our friendship breaking up, but that was the last straw. In the days following, one of her friends repeatedly texted me asking me to return and talk things out with my roommate. I said no way! Turns out, that woman ended up moving in with my old roommate, and I ran into her last year. She told me that I was right, and that she was completely awful. She apparently been dying her hair a lot in their apartment and got a stain on the carpet. Her new roommate came home to find her painting the carpet brown to try to cover the stains!

At this point, these stories just make me laugh, but oh my, am I glad I just live with my boyfriend and dog now."

Before We Get Started . . .

Before we get into the thick of it, here is what I call a "tip sheet" that you should use as your reference sheet during your first couple months of college. You want to copy this page and keep it somewhere safe just in case you find yourself not speaking to each other by your sophomore year.

Tip #1 – Every Little Thing She Does Is Not Magic

What started out as a minor annoyance you did not think bothered you has, two months later, turned into the fingernails on the blackboard and bane of your existence. Gum chewing, hair twirling, snoring, constant sighing, you name it, and it will eventually get on your nerves. Unless you are in a six-person suite and can actually move around from room to room, you are stuck in the same space with this person, and it is a small one at that. Did your mom ever tell you that patience is a virtue? You may not care if it is a virtue or not, but it is an attitude you will need to develop to accept your roommate and all of his or her faults. Keep in mind you will have yours as well.

Tip #2 – You Mean It Isn't Just About Me?

In addition to being patient, you will have to be tolerant and considerate of another person. It sounds like a lot to ask, but you would want the same from him or her. Leaving your clothes on the floor, putting an empty milk carton back in the fridge, and blasting YouTube from your PC while your roommate is sleeping does not apply.

Tip #3 – When Is a Guest Not a Guest?

You may think you "own" one-half of the room and can have anyone you want over any time of day as long as he or she stays in your half of the room. It doesn't quite work that way. Be considerate of your roommate's privacy, especially if you plan to do more than study with your guest. Ask first before inviting anyone to stay over. If you work out an agreement to do so once a week, your roommate should have the same option.

Tip #4 – Conflict Happens

You will, at some point, argue with your roommate, just as you argue with your family, loved ones and, some day, a partner or spouse. Do not hold a grudge for more than a day. Talk it out—do not think you can resolve conflict by text messaging and smiley faces. A conflict may seem overwhelming when it happens, especially when hurt feelings are involved, but in a few years, you may not even remember your roommate's name. Do not assume moving to another dorm will solve your problems. There could be a worse roommate looming right around the corner.

Tip #5 – Cleaning Fairies Don't Exist

Do not wait for each other to clean your room. Unless the cleaning fairy pops in on weekends, you both have to share the responsibility, so get over your opposition to operating a vacuum or working a mop and get moving. If a cleaning schedule will work and keep you both on track, switch off responsibilities week to week. If you absolutely cannot live without dusting every Saturday, and your roommate lives to scrub the sink, stick with the same jobs, everything will go smoothly, and your room will sparkle.

Tip #6 – Duck and Cover

Be ready to experience conflict with your roommate. Before moving in, do a very honest evaluation of yourself. What's your economic background and how does this influence your attitude? Are selfish or selfless? How do your perceive cultures different from your own? How tolerant are you?

You'd be surprised at the little things that may set people off (things you perceive to be little that are of great importance to others). Above all, be mindful and get to know your roommate really well.

Living Learning Communities (LLC)

Living Learning Communities provide settings where student academic success is supported through residential experiences. A floor or section within a residential hall is specifically designated for students who share common interests or academic majors, and feature programs, social activities, field trips, and other recreational activities that promote the particular community. The staff assigned to the community may be experienced in the area of interest or major, and helps students plan programs and activities. That staff person, or others assigned under his or her supervision, can also help new students adjust to university life and answer questions about classes, building locations, policies, and resources. LLCs provide opportunities for students to build strong relationships with peers with whom they share similar interests.

Sharing similar interests on the outset may also reduce the likelihood of conflicts with your roommates. Although you could still have opposite sleep or study habits, or be in a "neat versus slob" situation, you will at least have the bond of common interests, which could serve as a foundation for constructive dialogue when conflict arises.

Priority for placement within an LLC may be reserved for students enrolled in the academic program affiliated with that community. For example, to live in a performing arts LLC, you may have to be formally enrolled in a music, theatre or dance program. However, there are many LLCs that are not associated with an academic program, such as a "quiet" or "alternative-gender" LLC.

Examples of LLCs are diverse, and there are numerous opportunities to live in a community that fosters student involvement and shared experiences. If you are interested in an LLC and it is not listed on the university's housing website, contact the office. There may be a list of other students who are looking for the same LLC as you, and you could be the catalyst for starting a new community.

Many LLCs involve not only Resident Advisors (RAs) and Resident Directors (RDs) but also faculty members and local business leaders who provide individualized attention to students seeking career guidance. LLCs can also offer a free professional-speaker series, resume-building workshops, house dinners, and beneficial freebies.

Here is a sample of the kind of diverse LLCs offered at universities around the country:

- By major

- Community service

- Social justice

- French- and Spanish-speaking communities

- Cross-cultural education

- Global living

- Outdoor adventure

- Rainbow house (gay, lesbian, bisexual, transgender)

- Chicano/Latino cultural studies

- Black/African-American scholars

- Women in science and technology

Students Who Need Extra Care

The housing office works in conjunction with the office of disability services to offer options for students requiring disability-related housing accommodations. Wheelchair access and other barrier-free spaces can be arranged upon request, and universities have separate printed guidelines available in the office.

Universities host students from hundreds of countries each year and have designated departments, offices, and staff to assist international students in getting acclimated to their new country, university, and home away from home. Most residence halls welcome both American and international students, while others may have designated buildings or floors just for foreign students.

If you have any food allergies, you should have contacted the university before even applying to be certain their food services operations can accommodate your needs, including a specially designed menu and segregated eating areas, especially for peanut allergies. Be sure to tell your roommate about any food allergies. If you use an EpiPen, show your roommate where you keep it and explain to him or her how to use it in case of an emergency.

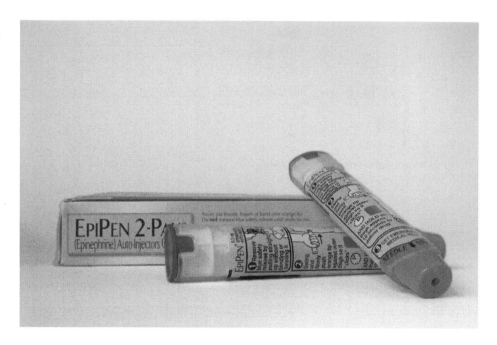

The number of young people and college students who suffer from asthma and allergies has increased dramatically over the past decade. Small living quarters, mold, and dust mites trigger allergy symptoms and, for some students, lend to a life-threatening living environment. Students suffering from allergies should contact the housing office at their university well in advance of the application process to find out what its policy is on allergy-proof rooms. They must also be absolutely certain they are not matched with a smoker or a roommate who may not smoke but socializes in smoke-filled venues at which smoke will be absorbed in his or her clothing. Many times, the school will be able to accommodate their needs, but they must act early. Dorms that have central air pose less of a problem, but if the university needs to accommodate special needs, early contact is crucial. It is also advisable that students check in with health services upon arrival so they have a record of their medical needs. Another resource may be the university's office of disabilities. If you use an inhaler or other asthma medication, show your roommate where you keep it and be sure he or she is aware of your condition should you need emergency help.

The Allergy and Asthma Network Mothers of Asthmatics (**www.aanma.org**) posts helpful information for college-bound students on how to navigate dorm living. It suggests students with asthma obtain an updated, written management plan from his or her allergist before leaving for college. It also suggests that dorm rooms are clutter free, with no upholstered furniture or secondhand rugs, an air filter, encased bedding, and regularly scheduled vacuuming and dusting. Asthmatic students and their parents should also know the location of the nearest hospital.

Chapter 2

Once You're There

Drawing a Line in the Sandbox: Claiming Your Territory

Have you ever watched *The Real World*? If not, you might want to watch a few episodes—not only to see what the most obnoxious roommate on the face of the planet looks like, but also to see him claim the first bed he sees without consulting anyone else. This is even before introductions are made. Not a good way to make friends.

The hope is that you will be assigned reasonable roommates who understand that compromise is key, and this includes the moment when everyone claims his or her space. If you do not care where your bed is, tell your roommate. This will make it easier for a roommate who may have particular reasons why she wants a bed near the door or against the wall. Just like living with your family, everyone will have his or her quirks.

Wait until everyone is in the room and after introductions are made. If possible, wait until parents have said their good-byes so they are not part of the decision-making. Remember, whichever space you claim is not a permanent decision. You can come up with a schedule to alternate spaces every semester or year.

Before packing in your entire room, remember: this is won't be Buckingham Palace. You have approximately 10 by 10 feet to work with. Also, if you brought an item that will not fit in your room or closet, ask your parents to take it back home.

Use your closet to hold as many items as possible. You want to do this for two reasons: so you can find what you need quickly and so that you are not tossing your clothes, shoes, and anything else on the floor. Your closet may have just a rod without any doors, sliding doors, or shutter-type doors that open out. Here are some handy strategies for making the most of the space:

- Over the door hooks and shelves are great space savers and don't require any holes, screws, or nails.

- Collapsible folding shelves are another great space saver since floor space is minimal. You can use them for textbooks, bike equipment, and beauty and health items.

- To even better utilize shelf space, buy some stackable trays. They come in various sizes, and some lift up or slide out like drawers.

When it comes to décor, well, this is a tough one. Unless you paint a white line dividing the room in half, or unless you are lucky enough to be living in a suite with your own bedroom, you will be subject to your roommate's tastes in wall hangings, rugs, lamps, and everything else that may not appeal to your more sophisticated sense of style.

But remember, the space is just as much as yours as it is theirs. If they start encroaching on your space, you have every right to say something about it. Take liberties on your side of the room as much as you want: posters, pictures, calendars, and anything that make you feel cozy, comfortable, and ready for success. Make sure to establish what you're comfortable sharing and what you're not. In other words, now is the time to draw the line in the sandbox.

A Word for the Wise . . .

Don't just waltz in, toss your belongings on a bed, and claim it as "yours" the minute you walk into your dorm room. Be open to compromising with your roommates, and remember that you can always switch spaces every semester.

Meanwhile, Back at the Dorm . . .

The dorms are a *great* site for inspection. While you make friends, casually knock on their doors every once in a while, scope out their style and how they live. Who knows, you two might be watering two complementary geraniums and go thrifting every Sunday for that retro art you love so much. ■

I Thought the Planets Revolved Around Me?

Adulthood is about becoming like your parents in unexpected, surprising, and sometimes disturbing ways. College is usually the initial step in this process, a time when you learn several crucial lessons and skills:

- To discard the idea that you are the center of the universe.

- Consider and respect the feelings and thoughts of others.

How much of the college experience is about you? All of it, you say? If your parent(s) are paying for any portion of your college tuition, room, and board, then much is about them. You have an obligation to make college a success, even if along personally defined parameters.

You may be thinking: What? I have an obligation? I thought college was all about partying, staying up late, drinking, dating, and wearing my pajamas to class. Well, your parents are not paying you thousands of dollars to spend all your time like the Dude in *The Big Lebowski*. They're paying you to learn, study, work hard, and, last but not least, grow up.

Living with roommate will indeed help you grow up. It's much like being in a relationship. You have to take the bad with the good. These people will have their annoying habits, but so do you. You will not be able to have everything your way and will have to find a fair balance that allows your rights to be respected as well as theirs. Here are some strategies for breaking down your egoism whenever you start to feel those familiar feelings of righteousness, entitlement, and annoyance:

- When your roommate smacks her lips when she eats pasta and this sends shivers down your spine, remember that you possess qualities that likely have the same effect on others. You don't notice them because you're not the one being irritated by them!

- Treat your roommate with respect. Respect is the gel of society. Without respect, everything would dissolve before our eyes. Even if he or she is rude to you, silence is better than making low blows and making the argument work. It's your responsibility to make the arrangement work.

- Take care of yourself. The best way to fulfill your obligation to your parents is to take care of yourself. This meaning detoxing on alcohol. Studying instead of partying. Exercising instead of pigging out.

R-E-S-P-E-C-T

This leads us to our next point: respect.

Picture Aretha Franklin belting out the song "R-E-S-P-E-C-T." She is a woman in charge, and you do not want to mess with her. She demands respect.

The same goes with mutual expectations of your roommate and yourself. You should respect their space, privacy, belongings, lifestyle, and desire to get the best education they can. They should do the same for you. If all roommates followed this guideline, there would be no reason for me to write this section, or perhaps even this entire book, as everyone would be respectful of everyone else. Peace, love, and flowery fields, right?

You may or may not be surprised, but disrespect is everywhere. Americans are admittedly and notoriously considered rude, hyper-competitive, and self-obsessed by people from other cultures, and this certainly comes into play in a living situation. Especially when the people in those situations don't have a lot of life experience, and thus, have not had many opportunities to learn.

Here are some scenarios, drawn from a general pool of experiences, and the strategies students have used to deal with them.

1. *He doesn't respect my wish to study.* He thinks college is one giant party but my parents have shelled out tens of thousands of dollars for me to go here. **I am transferring next semester to an honors dorm where students take studying seriously.**

2. *She doesn't respect the fact that this is my room too.* She rotates boyfriends and thinks I don't know they're having sex in my bed when I'm in class

or at work. I can't tell you how many times I came home and my bed was a mess. **I've complained to my RD, and she's being reassigned to a different floor.**

3. *He doesn't respect my right to peace and quiet.* Evidently, my roommate has never heard of headsets. He said he likes the "full effect" of hearing music blasted all day through a giant set of speakers. I will study in the library or in a friend's room, but why should I always have to accommodate him? **I complained to the RD, and he now must wear a headset when listening to music. He's not happy with me, but frankly, I don't care.**

4. *She doesn't respect my things.* My roommate assumes it is all right to use my shampoo, soap, and hair products. I don't know where she got this from because we actually set up a written agreement at the beginning of the year that neither of us wanted to share our things. The first time I pointed this out to her, she laughed at me. **When I locked my shampoo in my closet, she had the nerve to ask me where it was. I told her I had run out and that she would have to buy her own. When she saw it in the shower the next day, after she bought her own, she got the message.**

5. *He doesn't respect my political (religious) beliefs.* I'm a Christian and get up early every morning to pray. Sometimes a group of us on the floor prays in the game room while everyone is still sleeping. I'm not bothering my roommate, but he makes fun of my "God groupies." I don't know what his religious preference is, but I told him that his jokes aren't funny and they not only hurt my feelings, but also insult my family. **When I asked him how he would feel if someone insulted his family that put an end to his remarks. Now when I joke and ask him if he'd like to join our group, we both have a good laugh.**

The old adage about treating them as you would like them to treat you holds true when it comes to respecting the person (or people) you room with. Think about how you want to be treated, and treat them, their belongings, and lifestyle in the same way. When you study abroad, you don't want to be that childlike, selfish American that induces a groan among all the locals. You certainly don't want to create a hostile atmosphere in your living situation, where conflict is always ripe because you disrespected your roommate, used his or her stuff without permission, made fun of something they value, or are just consistently a hot mess.

A Word for the Wise...

Create a constitution for your room. Maybe get a little corny, make a poster, and hang it up as a constant reminder. The title could be "Respect" and a list of all the things that demand consideration and care in your living situation: reciprocity, mutual kindness, a respect for personal preferences, etc.

Meanwhile, Back at the Dorm . . .

The same advice goes for your dorm-mates. It may be even more crucial to demonstrate respect in the dorms, because there you have the potential to be shunned not by one, but perhaps 30 or more people! ∎

CASE STUDY: NAVIGATING THE FIRST YEAR OF DORM LIFE

Rebekah Slonim
Hillsdale College

I was a home-schooled introvert heading off to college four hours away from home, where I would be living with my best friend, Elisabeth, in the freshman girls' dorm with community bathrooms and tiny rooms. Several hundred feet away from this dorm — called Olds Residence — was McIntyre Residence, the only other freshman girls' dorm. Those rooms were larger and suite-style. But, since my soon-to-be roommate (who was extroverted) wanted to live in Olds, and because I was worried that I wouldn't make many friends in the dorm, I agreed that Olds was the better option.

Home-schooler leaving home for the first time. Rooming with my best friend. Noisy dorm. Community bathrooms. Rooms that were small even from a college dorm perspective. Recipe for disaster, right? Actually, no.

I look back on my freshman year as one of the best times of my life. But that wasn't inevitable.

Above all, the most important factor in having a positive roommate experience was that my roommate respected my boundaries.

I liked to study alone at my desk in the evening, and my roommate preferred to study in the library. The small room became incredibly cozy, so when my roommate eventually came back, I was energized by my time alone — and caught up with my homework — so I was ready to chat with her.

Worried that everything depends on being randomly assigned a boundary-respecting roommate? Remember that you need to *know* what your boundaries are beforehand. Self-knowledge is very important to a good roommate relationship. Otherwise, two months in, you suddenly realize that you're being pushed around and don't like it.

It also helped that we had similar sleep schedules — not too early, not too late. We would both generally be in bed by midnight or 1 a.m., and we would get up around 7 a.m. or 8 a.m. Another helpful factor was that we had comparable goals — both of us were very serious about our studies.

Even though my roommate was considerate, we still could have had serious conflict if her consideration of my needs and desires had not been accompanied with clear, honest, and mutual communication. I had a terrible habit of using dishes, stacking them up neatly, and then taking an eternity to wash them. Elisabeth objected to the smell — rightly so, of course.

Elisabeth would sometimes put her clothes on the ground and leave them there for a while. Or they would pile up on her seldom-used desk chair. I had never been accustomed to anyone doing that, and it seemed to clutter up the tiny space unnecessarily.

We both knew that the other person didn't like the habit, so we worked on it as much as we could. But mostly we just decided to look the other way. Some kind of irritation is going to develop if you live with anyone for any extended period of time. Just try to make it as insignificant as you can.

Some roommate success or failure is just dumb luck. If you've been polite and considerate and still had a bad experience, don't beat yourself up about it. Sometimes, you may get along fine with your roommate, but you're just never going to become besties. That's OK. But hopefully you *will* at some point get the chance to room with a friend who makes cohabitating a joy and delight because the benefits and memories truly are incomparable: a friendly word when you walk in at night or get up in the morning, encouragement before you take an exam, pleasant study breaks where you chat for a few minutes, actually being able to study together in companionable silence, walking to the dining hall together, and more.

When I think of my freshman year, I remember those things — not the inconvenience of the community bathroom or the piles of Elisabeth's clothes. I hope that can be true for you, too.

Most Common Complaints

East Coast, West Coast, private or urban university: no matter where you go, there are lists of common complaints that are universal to the roommate experience. The commonalities have little to do with the university or college itself, but with the realities of living in a small space with other human beings who initially are strangers.

We will examine each of these in detail in the following chapter, but here is the list, in no particular order:

- Different sleep and study habits

- Hygiene (or lack thereof)

- Cleanliness

- Respect for others' belongings

- Overnight guests

- Substance use

- Mental health issues

- Differences in cultural background, sexual orientation, and religious beliefs

- Room temperature (battles over thermostat)

- Noise levels

Here are some skills and strategies to keep in mind before you start living in a box with a stranger (no, it isn't *as* bad as it sounds!):

- *Keep your studies first and make adjustments if necessary.* If you end up with a roommate who leads a wild existence and could care less about getting a college education, be proactive. Move into an honors dorm or get on a waiting list for a single. The biggest conflicts arise when two people are completely mismatched when it comes to study habits.

- *Reflect on who you are instead of just focusing on the other person.* If you find yourself with a new roommate every semester, take a good, deep look at yourself. Maybe you are the problem. Maybe *you* are difficult to live with and always blame the other person. If you are the one moving from dorm to dorm, perhaps you have set up unrealistic expectations of what a roommate relationship is like.

- *Have reasonable expectations of people.* Even if they end up being your best friend, your roommate will have issues. They won't be perfect. They may end up liking other people more than you. Or, the person might be messier than you prefer. But are they *that* messy? Can you learn to just let go? Above all, your responsibilities are your only best friend forever. They will truly be there for you until they day you die. And the more you take care of them, the more you'll surround yourself with the people you like: successful, happy, motivated people who make the most out of life.

A Word for the Wise...

You will, at some point during your tenure as a college student, have a complaint about your college roommate. Many complaints can be easily dealt with by having an immediate conversation rather than assuming the problem will go away on its own. Communication is the key to a successful roommate experience.

Do Opposites Attract?

In physics, yes, opposites do attract. In real life, most of the time, they do not.

Yet we will consider the examples when opposites can form a symbiotic and happy relationship.

If you and your roommate have similar schedules, are either both neat or both sloppy, but have different majors, interests, and friends, that could be the formula for a successful relationship. Basically, as long as your primary living preferences are similar, you're bound to find a connection some way, even if you're the creative liberal and she's looking to climb the corporate ladder when she graduates.

This brings us back to the form. If you are the type of person who does not see a problem with stashing stale pizza crusts under your bed, but noted on the form that you are tidy and neat, then you'll wind up with someone who will very much resent you. Some students think that if they lie about being tidy, when they have never set foot in the same room as a vacuum cleaner, they will get matched with someone who cleans up for both of them just to avoid living in a swamp. Well, that person didn't go to college to become a swamp drainer.

You will, however, have a much smoother time with a roommate who lives like you, but possesses qualities that either intrigue or interest you. For example, if it's challenging for you to mingle at a social event, you may gravitate toward people who can walk into a room full of strangers and make small talk. It is also possible that you could acquire that particular trait by spending time with people who are naturally outgoing, just like it is possible you could pick up someone's accent by default because you are around him or her every day. In essence, many positive outcomes can arise from being around your opposite.

If the clash is deeply rooted, such as values you have, religious beliefs, or political views, and these issues surface on a regular basis, you will most likely not be able to resolve these differences—especially if you fundamentally don't respect them. While we covered respect as an important base for a relationship, you don't and shouldn't respect everything. For instance, what if your roommate continually disrespects people who look a certain way? What if he or she continually uses hateful and debasing language about women? Although you may say you respectfully disagree, you don't, and shouldn't, respect disrespect when you see it. This is the time to talk to your RD and see about another arrangement.

A Word for the Wise . . .

Opposite personalities, lifestyles, and backgrounds can teach you about a way of life different from your own, transform you, and help you develop new friendships.

Meanwhile, Back at the Dorm . . .

Maybe you have a perfectly respectful roommate. Roses, violets, and gardenias, right? Yes and no. You're bound to meet a disrespectful person in your dorm. If it gets out of hand, you should talk to the RD. Who knows, you could be saving *their* roommate from a year of misery. ∎

Communication, Communication, Communication!

Besides glaring examples of disrespect, most differences can be worked out with good communication. While you may think of good communication as endlessly listing your problems, this is undoubtedly false. Whether you're the neat freak or he or she is a different personality type, the best strategy you can use in communicating a problem is considering the following question before you begin a big talk:

"Is what I'm about to say kind, honest, and necessary?"

If it's at least two of the three, then you have every right to say what you need to say. If it's only one, *fugetaboutit*! For example, maybe it's honest for you to say "You're a pig, dude!" but did you *have to say that in order to get your point across* and in such a rude way? No. Maybe their mess is starting to encroach on your part of the room. You could say something that's necessary, kind, *and* honest: "You know, I enjoy living with you, but the mess on my side of the room is starting to irritate me."

This way, you're encouraging the person to grow (kindness), being upfront about how you feel (honest), and you're sticking up for yourself (necessary). Didn't that feel nice?

Dorm Staff and How They Can Help

Resident directors, assistants, and hall staff are there to make your experience as positive as they can. While they are obligated to follow and implement policies and guidelines (many of which they helped develop), they are there to assist you, answer questions and most of all, ensure your safety and well-being while living in their dorm. Talk to them about conflict. Not only do they have experience as a college roommate, but also they live in your dorm and have firsthand experience with conflict and common issues. Take advantage of their expertise and think of them as a valuable resource. Do not go to the dorm-mates first and discuss the problem. That is unfair to your roommate and can make the situation worse.

The housing staff that lives in your residence hall may have different titles, but share the responsibilities of overseeing day-to-day operations. Resident directors, "RDs," supervise other staff and are responsible for life within your residence community, overseeing matters related to facilities and assisting residents when there is a problem. Directors hold either a master's degree or are pursuing a graduate degree. They are supervised by someone who works directly within the housing office and who has professional experience in residence hall management.

RDs monitor activities and events taking place within your residence hall and enforce the code of conduct. Directors also supervise the resident assistants, or RAs: individuals who live on each floor. Assistant area coordinators and area coordinators are also full-time, live-in professional staff members in supervisory positions. They are all a valuable resource for students. They know the campus inside out and can help get you acclimated and find your way, both as a student and resident of the university community.

Desk Assistants are student workers who man the 24-hour front desks and are responsible for checking ID cards, signing in guests, and answering phones. In the case of a 3 a.m. emergency, this is the person you would call or go to. Some universities also have resident hall governments, which are organizations that encourage students to apply leadership skills and develop a productive and active community environment in your dorm.

You should only take a problem beyond the dorm staff when they have not been able to offer a viable solution. This would mean going to the director of housing the vice president for student affairs.

As will be discussed in later chapters, they may also refer you to the counseling center in instances where you or your roommate could be experiencing emotional problems outside the scope of what they can help with.

Chapter 3

The Common Irritations

You are stranded on a desert island. It is just you, some squawky birds, and swaying palm trees. But then you remember that in your pocket is a small guidebook, wrapped in plastic, entitled *Surviving Dorm Life: Skills and Strategies*. Let us also assume that you are starting college in two weeks and will need to master the concepts within this book in order to be eligible to get off that island and back to the land of iPhones and internet.

You pull the guidebook out of your pocket. It is a bit soggy, but still legible. You review the table of contents and are surprised at some of the topics covered. They seem obvious, you pass the test, and there you go: you're off the island and ready to set sail. But once you physically get to your dorm room, you're out there in the sea, which is the *true* test of your wisdom. That's why it's not important to rush through the guide, take a quick test, and set sail, but to truly master the concepts and understand their importance. Here are a few general guidelines of what you'll find in the following sections:

- Hygiene counts.

- You may fall in love at some point, but that does not mean your room-mate feels the same way about your partner. Work out overnight arrangements with your roommate *before* you work them out with the love of your life.

- Do not use the floor as your personal recycling area. Put dirty clothes and smelly sneakers in a container. Put food waste in the trashcan and empty it on a regular basis.

- If you did not pay for it, do not assume it is yours. Work out a sharing agreement *before* you eat those chips or "borrow" some shampoo.

- Do not room with your best friend from high school. It is not high school any more.

- Do not assume you can drink or do drugs because you are in college. Some people go to college to *learn*.

- If your roommate is not a fellow substance abuser, it is not okay to use substances in your room. Period. Plus, you can get expelled from your residence hall.

If you are having a problem with a roommate who takes a nap at 10 p.m. and then studies until dawn, and you did not indicate on your preference form that you are an early riser —even though there was a checkbox for that — well, Houston, we have a problem.

These are the common points of contention that you'll need to really think about as you navigate the testy waters of dorm life in college. The rest of this chapter will lay out why you shouldn't take them for granted as you laugh on the deserted island, ignorant to the storm that's about to brew in the deceptively calm waters.

Hygiene Primer

No one wants to admit he or she could be the problem when it comes to hygiene or lack thereof. We are all part of the human species. We are not made of plastic and have to come to terms with the fact that we live with other humans; humans have body odor, bad breath, stinky feet, smelly clothes, and gross habits, like flossing while your roommate is eating dinner.

However, when you are sharing a cramped space with one, sometimes two other people, poor or excessive hygiene (think strong perfume) can cause insurmountable tension, hurt feelings, and resentment that can lead to a total breakdown in communication. Indeed, it can be a strong wind in an already tumultuous sea.

Here are some basic strategies that will keep you squeaky clean and out of trouble:

Keep your body clean

This may seem like a no-brainer, but unless you are in a single room or you are too sick to get to the shower, you should visit it every day. Perhaps your family tolerated your natural scent because they are related to you and love you no matter what, but roommates do not exhibit unconditional love. Especially for your B.O.

This can be a hard concept for some. In fact, there could be a personal belief tied around it, such as: "My body is my sanctuary. So I decide what I do with it." This is certainly true, but if you're not washing, you could very well be intruding on someone else's space. Although it's not a physical invasion of space, such as a pile of socks on their side of the room, a scent is just as real, and just as present.

Wash your clothes

The best way to keep *you* clean is to keep what you *wear* clean. When you lived at home, maybe you could heap your dirty clothes on the bedroom floor in the way a child builds a humongous fort around them. But again, unless you live in a single, there will not be room for any mountain-like structures in residence halls. If you visit your parents on the weekends, and they welcome your dirty laundry with open arms, keep it in a laundry hamper until then.

You are the only one who loves your perfume

Just as not everyone will love the smell of your armpit, just as many people may hate the smell of your new perfume. If you have left the room in the morning but can smell your perfume upon returning eight hours later, you may want to cut back before your roommate has to tell you to. As with anything, moderation is key.

Good environmental hygiene

Are you the kind of person who takes care of your appearance before organizing your backpack every day? You smell like a freshly picked daisy every day. Your clothes sparkle, and your hair shines. There is only one problem: dirt and clutter. You leave the dorm looking like royalty but live like a serf in your room. Every Monday, vacuum, dust, organize, clean, do laundry, and take out the trash. Remember that your compact mirror won't show the floor full of old papers and your roommate's disgusted expression.

A Word for the Wise . . .

People who take care of themselves attract better friends and positive experiences. By investing time into your personal appearance and immediate surroundings, you're telling the world that you value yourself, and it will value you that much more.

The Early Riser Versus The Late Sleeper

Before I went to college, I reminded myself that Benjamin Franklin woke up at the crack of dawn, dipped that feather in the ink-bottle, and set to work. I told myself I would stop going to bed close to the time that he woke up. But then I realized that I wasn't Benjamin Franklin, that I lived in the age of the internet and endless distractions, that I had the essence of a vampire, and no matter when I went to bed, I could never wake up earlier than 6:30 a.m. Indeed, if I ended up with Benjamin Franklin as a roommate, I would be pretty upset at the considerable age gap, his eating habits, and being woken up an hour or two after I'd fallen asleep.

This is one of the most important reasons why it is important to be truthful on your roommate preference questionnaire. If you have planned your class schedule so they all take place early in the day but your roommate, who is a night owl like me, has scheduled his classes for late afternoon and evening, someone is not going to get the sleep he or she needs.

You will not *always* have control over your class schedule and it will most likely fluctuate from semester to semester. If you are in different "time zones," flexibility, understanding, and patience are necessary to keep things running smoothly between you.

If you are able, work out a rotating schedule. If John is up at 6 a.m. to study before class and you did not get home from work until 11:30 the night before, perhaps he could study in the library or lounge in the morning so you can get enough sleep. However, accommodating your late night schedule gets a bit tricky.

You will eventually have to come back to the room late at night. Even if you're quiet as a mouse, it is likely you will make some noise coming in. Add a third roommate, and the situation gets even more challenging.

In this scenario, there are two opposite class and sleep schedules. Both you and John get along, are good students, and do not want their varied schedules to interfere with their living arrangement. A few strategies to work around this dilemma are:

- *Buy earplugs.* Seriously. Pilots, flight crews, and business travelers use them all the time in hotels to drown out street noise, especially in major cities.

- *Buy a sleeping mask.* They have come a long way since the one Grandma used to use. Some even contain soothing eye gel. You can get a good night's sleep and ward off wrinkles at the same time!

- *Listen to sounds of nature on your iPod as you go to sleep.* There are a wide array of relaxing sleeping sounds: trains in the night, desert winds, waterfalls, rain on the window, swamp sounds, and more available on YouTube. When your roommate comes in late and you have an early class, you will not even notice over the sounds of a far off coyote howl in the Mojave Desert.

- *Discuss.* Before you guys pick your classes, talk about the best possible scenario for both of you.

- *Make a tough decision.* If this becomes, or remains, a source of ongoing conflict and you know the situation will not change the following year, or the year after, discuss if one of you should volunteer to move in with another roommate who has a similar schedule. This is a last resort because your new roommate could have a schedule agreeable with yours one semester, but then not the next.

- *Learn to live with it.* If things are otherwise good between you and your roommate and you have heard horror stories from friends about students who jumped from one roommate to the next, you could end up with the roommate from "hell" rather than one whose only fault was to get up early for class.

CASE STUDY: NOT-SO-SWEET DREAMS

Matt Sherer
U.C. Santa Cruz

Matt Sherer is a story producer living in Los Angeles, California. He advises all students not to just coordinate sleeping schedules, but to ask your roommate the very real question: Do you suffer from night terrors that are comparable to scenes from The Exorcist?

Back in school I lived a five-bedroom house with nine people. Because there were only five bedrooms, some of us shared a room. My roommate's name was Jimbo (no, it wasn't). I'd lived with Jimbo in an on-campus residence before though never shared a room with him. I knew him well, though, and the price was right to live in a double room with him.

As our group finalized the living arrangements, Jimbo took me aside and told me that he had something called "night terrors." He mentioned that he didn't have them often, but when he did, it meant that he'd sometimes yell in his sleep, sleepwalk, or just have bad nightmares. He didn't think it'd be a problem, and neither did I. I just synonymized "night terror" with "nightmare" and daydreamed about how I'd decorate my half of the room.

The nine of us moved in. Night one in the house was filled with laughs and warmth. Night two was similar. Jimbo was a good roommate and kept to himself mostly: he was also insanely neat and polite, which was a godsend. We had talked about putting up a partition, but we were comfortable with each other and collectively decided that it wasn't necessary. Jimbo and I dug a fire pit in our back yard.

Classes started, and Jimbo got stressed. His major was an intense one, and he juggled an off-campus job. I'd often be asleep or in bed by the time he came home. He liked to watch Netflix in bed with headphones on. I used to roll over and peek when his screen illuminated the dark room too much. Often enough, he'd be biting and sucking on his fingernails as he watched TV. He must've not realized how loudly he sucked on them because the smacking noises would keep me up — and I sleep with earplugs.

One night I must have been in a deep sleep because I hadn't noticed Jimbo come in and turn on Netflix. Then at about 3 a.m. a blood-curdling murder scream wakes me up. I wish you could have heard it. It came from Jimbo's bed. It was the scariest thing I've ever heard. My heart almost burst through my throat. I couldn't see Jimbo, but I blurted, "Are you OK?" His voice, delayed, responded sleepily: "Yeah . . . what? Huh? Mmm . . . " Jimbo went back to sleep. I didn't.

The next morning, I talked to some of my housemates about Jimbo's scream. My housemate Joaquin thought Jimbo was being murdered. Someone else thought she imagined it. I brought it up to Jimbo later, and he couldn't remember screaming. He apologized for the scream, of course, but he had no idea how much it scared me.

Stupidly, I continued to live in that house with Jimbo. I'd go on to experience at least a dozen more night terrors while Jimbo continued to forget them.

Meanwhile, Back at the Dorm . . .

Did you know that you not only have a roommate, but also dorm-mates that can hear you in the hall? Usually, the RDs institute quiet hours, which usually go from 10 p.m. until 6 a.m. This means for night owls: don't crack up with your friends in the hallway, and keep it down. For early risers, close the doors softly and don't slam down your things in the shower. ■

Noise Is Just That: Noise!

It is highly likely that you will, at some point, live with a roommate who keeps the TV on all day or considers blasting classic rock a study tool. Noise is an incredibly common cause of conflict between roommates. Most preference questionnaires include a section on whether the student prefers complete quiet, low music, loud music, or television while studying. If you have a strong preference, this is the time to make it known. Many dorms even have quiet floors and Living Learning Communities for people who like to live in an almost library-like setting. If you're going for honors, this may be your best bet.

Other people just like it loud. That's how some people are naturally: their voice, their mannerisms, and the surroundings in which they grew up. Others may not be "loud" most of the time, but talk constantly on their cell phone without regard to anyone around them or play their MP3s at high volume so a person 10 feet away can hear. If you're one of either kind of people, respect the people who live like they're in a temple, and pick a roommate who lives like a rock star. Maybe your guitar playing sounds like the *Rolling Stones* to you, but it could sound like children playing in a sea of Styrofoam to another.

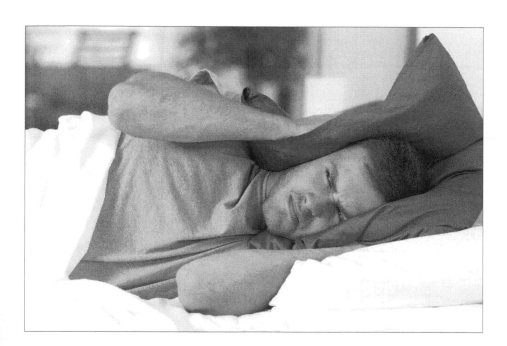

When Guests Overstay Their Welcome

Sooner or later, a guest becomes an obligation.

I remember in arts camp, during my first prolonged roommate experience, I stayed with two other roommates at the interesting age of 16. One of them had a friend who was a year younger, and thus significantly less mature. I bought our roommates a big cake as a good-bye gift, and she ate a significant portion of it without asking. This is called "overstaying your welcome."

It is very possible that at some point along the road, you or your roommate will have a guest who overstays their welcome. A new girlfriend or boy-friend will come along, an old friend or sibling will want to spend the night, or your dorm-mates will want to hang out with you in your room. Usually, you and your roommate can work out a schedule. But there are scenarios where one or the other will just assume everyone will be "cool" with the situation. Many, it seems, are not.

This is an important matter to discuss before inviting overnight guests. Do not wait until you come back to your room after a day of classes and find a coded note on the door, such as "Do Not Disturb. We're Studying." It's important to establish a policy before it comes to that point.

It takes skill and a firm hand to lay down the law, in a sense.

Following are some guidelines for this vital conversation.

Are there specific nights of the week you don't want overnight guests?

You may have an early and difficult class on Friday, and so want to get to bed early the night before. You may have told your roommate last week that you were having a guest over the following Saturday, but she invited someone for the same night after you had made plans.

Are there certain people in particular who make you uncomfortable when they visit or stay over?

If a friend or guest of your roommate's has ever acted in a threatening manner, or if you have felt harassed by that person, you should not tolerate that behavior. As difficult as it may be to tell your roommate this, you have every right to speak out. If your wishes are not respected, tell your RD. There is zero tolerance for threatening behavior or harassment on college campuses.

Is it all right for the guest to use your personal items? Share your food? Use your computer?

The answers can only come from you. Set boundaries and make your wishes known. Do not assume your roommate will know your wishes if you have not shared them with her. (Here is a hint: The answer should be "no." It is not all right for the guest to use any of your personal items. That is why they are "personal.") This is part of the "overstaying their welcome."

What is the arrangement for planning an overnight visit?

You may want to work out a weekly schedule in advance. If your roommate has his girlfriend over every Friday and Saturday night throughout the semester, that is not fair to you. Even if you are not in a relationship, you may still want quiet time on the weekend. If a family member is in town for a few days, work that into the schedule. Again, respect and cooperation with each other will make the planning go more smoothly.

What is off limits when it comes to overnight guests?

If you are abstinent, do not drink alcohol, or are opposed to drugs, say it now, or it will be harder to address later. For example, if you have religious beliefs that promote abstinence, tell your roommate in a manner that is non-threatening or judgmental. Tell her that you have made a decision to abstain from sexual behavior and that you hope she will respect that. This does not mean she will because it is your belief and not hers, but at least you have made your position known.

Are there certain times of day you don't want visitors?

When thinking about how often you have guests over, don't *just* include overnight guests, as the dorms will likely have their own policy on how many times a person can stay the night. Think about all the guests you have during the day. Are you and your friends always studying in your room, and you notice your roommate promptly packing his or her things and heading out? Conversely, do you have a social butterfly as a roommate who hosts small parties for the dorm-mates every day?

The Third Wheel

When your roommate gets a partner, you may find that you suddenly have an additional, and unwelcome, roommate. This can cause all kinds of conflicts, from disrupting sleeping and study schedules to jealousy, miscommunication, and problems with university housing guidelines, which will include a policy on overnight guests.

This is also a tricky situation because even though the university has rules regarding overnight guests, you probably do not want to report your roommate to the RD. This will not make you the most popular student on the floor, and the tension between the two of you will be close to unbearable. Then what do you do?

If you feel you are always being asked to leave the room to accommodate their "own private time" (which, as it turns out, is not so private), stand up for your rights. If you continue to accommodate their requests, your roommate will assume you are ok with the situation. Even though you do not have the right to tell her who she can have over or whether she can be in a relationship, you do have the shared rights of your living space.

Speak directly to your roommate about this and work out a fair agreement. If you go home most weekends, let her know you have no problem with him staying over while you are not there. If you have a good friend down the hall, offer to spend one night a week there — but only if you are fine with this arrangement.

Similar conflicts can arise if your roommate has a best friend who spends a lot of time in your room, as we referred to earlier. Your privacy is affected, and so is your quiet study time.

If you need to have a conversation with your roommate about the unwelcome boy/girl/best friend, here are some ways to approach it, depending on the level of the conflict.

If the situation is tolerable, but on some level is interfering with your schedule or you do not want the situation to escalate:

> "I'm really happy for you. Jim seems like a great guy, but I wonder if he could stay over Friday or Saturday night instead of Sunday. You know how anxious I get about that early Monday morning lab."

"Can we alternate weekends so each of us gets a few days to ourselves?"

If the situation is definitely interrupting your schedule and he or she leaves you notes to "come back later" — or asks you to study at the library instead of in your room — it is unreasonable for him or her to expect that you will accommodate those preferences:

"You know, Lisa, I don't mind Jim staying over one night a week, but he's been staying over three nights in a row. I need some privacy and quiet time during the week. So why doesn't he come over every other Saturday night?"

"Could you spend some time at Jim's instead of him always being here? It's just hard for me to study and have privacy when he's in the room so often."

"I don't think it's fair for me to have to stay out of my room because Jim is here. I think you would feel the same way if I constantly asked you the same thing, so we're going to have to work something out."

If the situation is intolerable and his or her presence is an ongoing disruption to your daily life, explain to your roommate that she or he needs to either work out a fair arrangement with you, or you will be forced to complain to the RD. He or she will not want that to happen any more than you do, so there is good chance your roommate will be willing to work something out.

Perhaps this goes without saying, but under no circumstances should you tolerate an overnight guest you are uncomfortable with or feel threatened by in any way. If this is the case, your well being is the first priority. Ask your roommate to speak to him or her in private and be clear with your message. Let your roommate know in no uncertain terms why his or her guest is not welcome. You should immediately voice your concern. Here are some conversation starters:

"Jim has made comments to me that are sexist and it makes me uncomfortable. I respect your right to hang out with whomever you want, I just don't want him here when I am in the room."

"I've expressed my feelings about using drugs, and I don't approve. You and Jim can make the choices you want, just take it outside of the room."

"I'm not comfortable with you bringing so many strangers to our room. I get it, it's college, we're meeting so many cute guys, but taking them back to the room might be better if you had a single. Since we're living together, I think we're going to work on finding a limit."

If at the end of all this, your roommate ignores your concerns and continues to have strangers over or a person who makes you uncomfortable, go to your RD. Your rights are being violated. Losing a friend is second to any harm that could come to you.

Sharing Is Caring! (But Not in this Case)

The decision to share belongings is one thing that has been previously covered, but what about sharing information about your roommate? If Marie's mother calls and you tell her she did not come home last night, you are setting up a situation that could result in a panic call to campus security with hysterical parents worried about their child.

There was a student I remember, Luke, who told me how his mother called, and his roommate told her, "Oh, Luke is still sleeping. He was out partying all night."

This is the point where I wish this were an audiobook, so you could hear the loud game show buzzer go: "*EHHHHHH!* Wrong! Wrong, wrong, wrong!"

It is not your responsibility to report your roommate's comings and goings unless your roommate is an incredibly talented toddler. If it's serious, like your roommate is harming himself or herself you would call the RD.

If you have information about your roommate's personal life that is confidential, or better for his or her sake not to share with anyone else, keep it to yourself.

How about personal belongings? There is room for negotiation when it comes to sharing, and that discussion should take place when you have that first conversation before move-in day. Do not bring two microwaves or two coffee pots. There will not be room for both of them anyway. As with many other topics covered in this book, communication is the key. If you make it clear how you feel about sharing personal items ahead of time, you will have taken the first steps to avoiding future conflicts. To provide some guidelines, here is a "discussion" list, which includes some items you may not want to share:

- Towels, washcloths, sheets, pillowcases

- Deodorant, hair products

- Combs, brushes

- Clothes

- Toothbrushes, toothpaste

- Makeup

- Perfume/cologne

- Jewelry

- MP3s, laptops, desktops, cell phones

Here is a list of items that could be up for negotiation:

- Small appliances allowed under the residence hall guidelines

- Televisions, radios

- Small furniture items

- Bookshelves

- Text books

- Snacks (as long as the cost is split)

- Toilet paper, paper towels, tissues (as long as the cost is split)

Meanwhile, Back at the Dorm . . .

You might end up having a lot of nice dorm-mates, with whom you could end up sharing a lot of great things! Try having a "snack potluck" every Friday where everyone brings his or her favorite snacks and watches a movie in the lounge. Or, better yet, pool in for a really awesome and decently sized coffeemaker and have coffee every Monday morning with your favorite dorm-mates. ∎

Locking Up

There are several million college students living in dorms across the country, which means there is a high potential for theft. The most commonly stolen items include jewelry, laptops, cell phones, MP3 players, textbooks, and cash. Items can be stolen by someone else living in your dorm, a guest one of your dorm-mates has signed in, or your roommate.

Someone once told me she repeatedly reminded her roommate, who grew up in a small town, to lock the door, even if she was just going down the hall to the bathroom. When someone stole her iPod, after her roommate left the room unlocked while in class, her roommate got into a huge fight with her, demanding to be paid back for her loss. (Luckily, her loss was covered under her parents' homeowners insurance.)

It is not only the safety of personal items you should be concerned about, but also more importantly your and your roommate's personal safety. You also do not know every guest a dorm-mate has signed in. In an ideal world college students could put complete trust in every other college student, but that is not the world in which we live. Your safety, and the safety of your roommates and hall mates, should be a number-one priority, no matter what the demographic or location of your college.

Do not assume a small, private, exclusive college is any safer than a large, urban university. Be mindful of this, and protect yourself and your roommates by always locking the door, even to run down the hall to microwave some popcorn. Keep a few keys on university "necklaces" on a hook by the front door. Just do not forget to put them back. This way, a key is always available for quick exits and entrances, and it is a visible reminder because it is right next to the door. You may want to label the keys with your names as well.

One last word on locking up: Do not, under any circumstances, ever lock your roommate out of her room. If you think it is a joke, it is not funny, and you could endanger that person. If you do it out of spite or revenge, you could (and likely will) have disciplinary action taken against you. If you do it because you have a guest and want some privacy, you have absolutely no right to keep your roommate from entering the room. It is hers as well as yours. She is paying as much as you are to live there.

Here are a few safety tips to keep your room and belongings secure:

Keep your valuables at home

If you must bring them to your dorm (passport, digital camera, jewelry) hide them. Many thefts happen within a few minutes, when you or your roommate runs down the hall to use the bathroom or microwave and do not lock the door. Thieves work like mountain lions: when they see an opportunity to hunt, they will go in for the kill. So just don't give it to them.

Keep an eye on your laptop

Laptops are one of the most commonly stolen items, and unless you carry it everywhere (the bathroom?), it can be stolen in less than a minute. The coffee shop is the easiest site for this to happen; you think, *people are watching, there's so many people, how could this happen?* I'll tell you what: one time, I must have been sitting seven feet away from a man's backpack at a library, and it was stolen right under my nose. Why? It's not *my* responsibility to take care of someone's stuff; it's just not on my mind! A student got his laptop stolen at a coffee shop where he knew virtually everyone there, and even worse, his only copy of his dissertation was on it, along with his back-up drive. Think twice before you take your laptop for granted.

Lock the door when you're not expecting guests

Need we say more?

Keep track of who comes and goes

This is important to notice not only from your room, but your floor. If someone suspicious is lurking around or acting strange, call the RA. Same goes if you see someone who looks and acts nothing like a college student.

If your roommate has someone in the room while you are at class, think twice about leaving your very pricey textbook on your desk or your brand-new jewelry in sight. You may get along great with your roommate and his or her company, but they are essentially strangers.

Meanwhile, Back at the Dorm . . .

You may feel like you are part of a family in your dorm, but the students are not family members. You may feel as though your dorm-mates have a common bond, but that does not mean one of them will not steal from you. Do not be naïve about what can or cannot happen in a college dorm. You may very well have mountain lions in your midst, and he or she will take advantage of your trust. ∎

A Word for the Wise . . .

College is expensive enough, and it's only getting pricier with each passing year. Do you really want to tack on thousands of dollars worth of lost belongings?

Step Up, Step Out, and Get Involved

In addition to the benefits of living in an LLC, there are many opportunities to be involved with your university outside your role as a student and roommate. College will be the most culturally rich environment you'll ever experience, encouraging new ideas, friendships, and learning experiences on a daily basis. Not only will extracurricular activities benefit your academic and social growth, but they will also provide "space" for you away from your dorm room and apart from your roommate.

In other words, you do not want to spend every free minute with your roommate, no matter how well you get along. Making a life outside of the dorm room will likely ease the impact of any of the "common irritations" covered in this chapter.

Extracurricular activities are a good way to get connected to the university and become part of a community outside classes and your dorm. If you are a commuter, part-time, or working student, you will have less time, but there are enough activities even at small colleges from which you can pick and choose. There are schools with hundreds of clubs, and even if you do not find one that matches your interest, you can approach the office of student affairs or housing and ask to start one.

A student I knew from school, Nikki, took up knitting during her sophomore year and found that, because of her full class load and part-time working schedule, it was the most convenient activity because she could do it anywhere on campus. She posted a notice in the student activities center, looking for other students who liked to knit. The response was so overwhelming that she ended up organizing a knitting group in five separate dorms!

The groups then connected with the office of international students and started a donation drive in which hand-knitted items were sent to children's homes in China.

On-campus jobs or internships are also a good way not only to meet new people, but also get involved with another academic area outside your major. I was linguistics major, but became an archivist for a professor in the Latin American/Latino Studies department, where I was responsible for sorting through thousands of documents from the '80s from activist organizations protesting the *contra* wars in Nicaragua. I learned so much about these inspiring people while meeting many of the people surrounding me in the department.

If you are encountering ongoing conflict with your roommate and can't move right away, being involved in extracurricular activities will give you the chance to spend time outside your room. Who knows, maybe you'll be so excited to be doing what you love, that your roommate won't get on your nerves as much.

A Word for the Wise . . .

Love is blind, not only to the flaws of the beloved, but also to other people's problems and annoyances. When you're doing what you love, the negative things that usually attract your attention will stop bugging you so much because you've got this awesome thing right in front of you!

CASE STUDY: WE JUST COEXISTED

Yvonne Bertovich
University of Florida

It seems to be some sort of universal guarantee that all college freshmen attending larger state schools must live on campus their first year. I honestly didn't hate the idea. I thought it'd be fun to be in the thick of it, immersed in a new place entirely so that I could get my bearings—not to mention I went without a car my first semester, too, and navigating the bus system still terrified me at that point. Suburban gals like myself aren't privy to bus rides.

Since I was staying in-state and attending the University of Florida, I had the option of rooming with someone I knew already, but I honestly wanted to branch out—at least a little bit. I remember feeling like an idiot when I posted a quasi-dating-site bio about myself in my graduating class' Facebook group in hopes of attracting a potential roommate. But, as a weak example of peer pressure, "everyone else was doing it." I joked around about my exotic-sounding name, my love of peanut butter, and how "more people than just my mom have told me I'm charming"—embarrassing, right? As luck (or a lack thereof, but I'll get into that later) would have it, a few girls reached out to me.

Fast-forward a little bit, and a girl named Jamie and I had officially agreed to be roommates. We would be sharing a double room (two beds, one room, community bathroom) in Jennings Hall, one of the arguably nicer dorms that UF had to offer.

To say that Jamie and I were excited to have "met" and become roommates in a few short months was an understatement. Our relationship (gag) flourished over Facebook and text. We Snapchatted almost every day about everything from stupid selfies to our gripes about still being in high school and how we couldn't wait to graduate. We bonded over a wide variety of things: our weird humor, our Christian faith, our less-than-stellar opinion of rushing a sorority, being active, and spending time outdoors. I'm pretty sure we both thought we were going to be best friends.

If you haven't caught onto the slight bitterness in my nostalgia, I'll lay it out for you right now — things were not great. We did not become best friends. When we moved out of our dorm at the end of freshman year, we both left silently and at different times, and we didn't even attempt to say goodbye. We haven't talked since, and our paths miraculously haven't crossed.

So, what happened? I'm not entirely sure. It was just a very, very weird situation — which I realize is a pretty sucky explanation. When we moved in, we tried to hang out with one another and include each other in plans. I felt awkward going with her anywhere, and I felt unwelcome whenever I spent any small amount of time with her when she'd seldom include me. She was cold, quiet, and hard to read. I soon realized that any effort I was putting into trying to forge a real, in-person friendship with her was a waste. I felt ignored, avoided, and alone even though we lived five feet from one another. Of course, we never confronted one another. We once went three weeks without saying more than "hey" to each other. We never fought. We never really had fun either; we just coexisted.

I guess I should thank her, though, because the gym became my sanctuary my freshman year. As horrible and weird and tense as it was in my room — my "home" — these feelings were completely eclipsed by the happiness and solitude I experienced while exercising. I would go to the gym or walk for hours (and still do).

Now, I'm in my junior year, and I've spent the last two years an entirely, uncharacteristically joyful compared to freshman me. I live in an apartment not far off campus, and I have had several different roommates. I have had nothing but great experiences (or at least better ones). I'm not saying that I was unhappy strictly because I lived in a dorm, and I'm not saying that I always love apartment life either. All I'm saying is that college teaches you a lot about yourself because you're constantly being tested — figuratively, literally, emotionally — and it's completely horrible and awesome all at the same time.

Chapter 4

The Personality Spectrum

If you become a parent, you may spend more time with your child's friends than your own. You will be witness to a spectrum of personality traits, from incessant whining to perpetually runny noses to the constant threat: "I am telling your mom." You will see some of the same traits in college roommates, except the list gets longer and the conflicts more difficult to resolve. Unfortunately, "Here's a lollipop" stops working at some point.

Before we go into the major "camps," shall we say, here is a long list of different college-personality "archetypes" to show you just how diverse they can be:

The Converter: This person tries to convert his roommate to change diet, religion, political views, or recycling habits. The end result will be an annoyed roommate leaving cheeseburger remains, Rush Limbaugh books, and empty soda cans in the room to get the message across that conversion is not an option.

The Natural: This person wears hemp clothing, follows the European approach to hygiene and razors, and has Woodstock posters on the walls.

The Animal: Have you seen the movie *Animal House*? Do you remember the character played by John Belushi? Enough said.

The Geek: This is the student who studies every free minute, only socializes with other gamers (and does so on an online RPG), and is shunned by other groups of students. We've all seen him in the cartoons.

The Slacker: This person sleeps through classes, gets high every day, and wears shorts and flip-flops in January (in Buffalo). There's a hidden genius in there . . . somewhere, we hope.

The Caffeinator: This person cannot go to the bathroom without a cup of coffee. She is probably an addict, but effectively disguises this with "coffee snobbery." You've never tried an Ethiopian roast, you say? Well, you might as well not be living.

The Communicator: This person constantly talks on her cell phone, relating the most mundane events to friends ("I just took a bite of ramen. What are you doing?"). It's almost like there's no meaning behind what she says, just pure sound. Her phone has become her grown-up teddy bear, and you swear you can hear her murmur "Goodnight, Phone-y" before she drifts off to sleep and gets a text a minute later.

The Blender: The most desired of them all! These are the people you want for roommates. They can adjust to almost any situation. They are good students, good children, well balanced, and mature, but can still have fun and take it all in with a grain of salt.

A Word for the Wise . . .

You will encounter a rainbow of personalities in college and throughout your life. Think about how dull it would be if everyone behaved the same and held the same beliefs, ethics, and views. Your experience as a roommate will better prepare you to deal with different personality types in your post-college life.

Meanwhile, Back at the Dorm . . .

Got the "Blender" as a roommate? Congratulations. But let's be real: you're in a dorm. You will have very frequent and intense contact with at least 30 other people (probably more, depending on the dorm size). Maybe the "Converter" doesn't annoy you as much, and you may even enjoy challenging her in a debate! Maybe it's the "Communicator" who really gets on your nerves. Do your best to avoid who you really, really can't stand and accept the rest. No one is perfect, not even the "Blender," so try to appreciate her strengths above her weaknesses. ■

Every Little Thing She Does Is *Not* Magic

If anyone reading this book has ended a romantic relationship, you will recall what it is like toward the end, right before the actual breakup. Everything he does annoys you. You can dissect the minutia of every sentence she utters to validate why you are breaking up.

The same goes for roommates who may be on opposite ends of the personality spectrum. She spends Saturday mornings cleaning, and you have not seen a rising time before noon on the weekend since sixth grade. Your breakfast menu consists of doughnuts and diet soda, and she eats raw vegetables. To annoy you even more, she offers you a bite each time, along with a subtle lecture on improving your eating habits.

To annoy her in return, you take a sloppy slug of your 24-ounce diet soda and follow up with a healthy burp.

Remember that some habits can be broken. Throwing dirty clothes on the floor may be a component of someone's personality, but that behavior can be changed through a non-accusatory conversation. Plus, that behavior affects everyone living in the same space: it clutters the room, creates an unwelcoming image, and could even result in unpleasant odors. These are behaviors that can be, and really should be, changed in a shared living arrangement.

Yet there are some fundamental things about a person that can't be, and shouldn't be, changed. You will have to navigate and accept some personality traits that drive you crazy. You cannot expect someone to change entirely to please you any more than you would appreciate him or her asking you to do the same.

For behaviors that can and should change, the best approach is to talk about it right away. You cannot bring about change by being silently resentful and angry. As you will read later on, use "I" and "you" whenever possible in a non-accusatory, respectful manner:

"Your gum snapping distracts me when I am studying. You may not be aware that you are even doing it. Could you not snap your gum? I would appreciate it."

"I would appreciate it if you did not leave your nail clippings on the bathroom floor."

The company "Nifty Notes" has a humorous "Roommate FYI" check-off list you can purchase and post in your room (search for "Nifty Notes" online for ordering information). Depending on your roommate's sense of humor, some of the check-off items on this list may provide a friendly reminder to your roommate that she shares a space with someone.

Some of the "nifty" check-off tips include:

- Stop whining

- Mind your own business

- Get over it

- Aim for the toilet

- Get out of the relationship

- Clean the toilet

- Ask first

- Pay me back

Probably not for the faint of heart — use wisely!

The Neatnik Versus the Slob

It's probably the most commonly heard complaint among housing directors, RDs, and college roommates. What you consider neat versus your roommate's point of view can create major conflict. If you both live as though you're in the middle of the aftermath of a hurricane, and neither seems to mind, that's great. You have found the perfect roommate!

It is the in-between, gray area when it comes to cleanliness that creates conflict. Whatever your tolerance is for order and cleanliness, you must clean your dorm room. Dirty clothes smell, as do dirty bodies, but that is covered elsewhere. You will be on the run constantly in college, going from class to class, job to class, and being able to find clean underwear without sifting through a mountain of junk will reduce your stress level.

Work out a schedule with your roommate. Type it out, print it, and post it where it is noticeable. If she does not mind vacuuming, assign her that task every week. Rotate jobs every other week or decide on keeping the same one. When you come up with a cleaning schedule, figure out a time and day that works well for the both of you. If someone is expecting family or friends to visit for the weekend, and your cleaning schedule is Monday night, take the initiative and clean before company arrives.

However, all of this is easier said than done. There is a good chance you will be matched with someone whose idea of "clean" does not meet your standards, or the other way around. Being overly organized can be a sign of Obsessive Compulsive Disorder. Sloppiness can also be a sign of depression (more on both of these later). Assuming your roommate suffers from neither, but just does not care where he tosses his smelly sneakers or other items, and you do, you have a conflict on your hands.

If you worked out a roommate agreement before moving in, you hopefully included an unofficial "cleaning" or "cleanliness" policy. If you, or your roommate, lied on your questionnaire about your level of tidiness, one of you is to blame when tension builds.

Let us assume you are faced with this dilemma: for whatever reason, you, the orderly, neat, loves-to-organize-clothes-by-color person, are matched with a roommate who considers cleaning moving a pile of dirty laundry from one corner of the room to another. The situation is not intolerable, but it annoys you. In other words, your nose is constantly assaulted by stench and your Febreeze can't hide it anymore (the fact that you bought Febreeze doesn't quite send the message to him, either).

You have a few choices. You can have repeated, calm, and mature conversations with him about respecting each other's space and see if his behavior changes. Let him know this is something that is important to you, but do not go off the deep end with cleanliness standards and cleaning instructions. Just let him know that you are a neat person (as you indicated on your questionnaire) and that you would hope he at least keeps his part of the room and shared space clean.

If you have a great relationship, and feel that humor is a good way to approach difficult topics with him, make a joke about how funny it is that you were assigned to live together when you are so opposite. It's almost like you guys should be on a reality television show. If that doesn't work, try to gauge the level of slobbiness. Is it tolerable? Is it something you can live with? This depends on how it directly affects you. If he is just tossing everything he owns in his closet, but keeping the door closed, there is no reason that you cannot live with this. But maybe his side of the room is just SO cluttered that it kind of depresses you. Make your feelings known, but follow the communication principle: "Is the way I'm presenting this necessary, kind, and honest?"

The Gossip

You have probably heard this from a teacher or parent at some point in your life: no one likes a gossip. Anyone at any stage in life can fall prey to gossip. Gossip is never warranted or deserved. At one time, gossip was only spread by word of mouth, but with unlimited access to the Internet and the speed at which gossip can be spread, there are more dangerous consequences. Young people have committed suicide because of the hurtful rumors and downright lies people can IM or text to friends or post online. One unwarranted rumor started by a student who has a gripe about another can spread like wildfire, and can be impossible to retract or refute.

If you find out your roommate is talking about you behind your back, you can confront her or choose to ignore it. Ignoring it may sound like the more reasonable reaction, but, in reality, it is difficult to do. Your instincts are to fight back and defend yourself. But by confronting your roommate and making it clear you know it was her and that you do not tolerate gossip puts her on the spot. If you do it immediately after finding out, you have a better chance of catching her off guard, as she has not yet starting justifying her actions to herself and others.

The best tactic to stop gossiping in its tracks is to **be direct**. This is not a time to worry about hurt feelings, especially if you are the person to whom the gossip is directed. Worrying about your popularity or losing friends only prolongs the opportunity for others to gossip about you or a friend of yours. State your position on gossip (you disapprove) to the person you know is doing the gossiping. Avoid name-calling, finger pointing, and the urge to "get back" by spreading gossip about the person you need to confront. Here are some ways to approach, or not approach, the person who is gossiping about you, a friend, or an innocent stranger:

Accusatory approach: "I know you were talking about me behind my back." This is an open-ended statement in that it gives the other person the perfect opportunity to deny it or act as though he or she has no idea what you are talking about.

Better approach: "Were you talking about me behind my back?" Now the other person has to respond with either "Yes," "No," "I have no idea what you're talking about," or "You're crazy/paranoid." If he claims he does not know what you are talking about, there is a good chance he does.

Other approaches (notice the use of "I" and "me," which are always useful when resolving conflict and making your feelings and position known):

"It hurts my feelings when *I* hear you are talking about me to other people."

"*I* do not tolerate gossip. It is hurtful and demeaning. *I* am sure you would not want people to talk about you behind your back."

"If there is something you want to say about *me*, say it to me rather than behind my back."

"When you talk about *me* behind my back, not only is it hurtful, but also it is unfair as *I'm* not there to defend myself."

If you choose to ignore gossip and it continues, it may eat away at you, and your resentment toward that person will only grow.

When it is not gossip, but you have some personal information about your roommate that you know would be hurtful, keep it to yourself. This is not only a good rule of thumb to follow as a college roommate, but in post-college life as well. If you happen upon information that you feel is either endangering your roommate's well-being, or would be emotionally damaging, and do not know what to do, think it through before telling anyone. The best bet would be to consult with your school's counseling service or share it with your RD.

Meanwhile, Back at the Dorm . . .

It would be a relief if you were just living with one other person in an apartment complex. I mean, where is that gossip going to go? You have no one to gossip to. Really, in that situation, it's advantageous to work it out because you want it to work out. In a dorm situation, though, alliances can form, enemies are made, and there is ample opportunity to gossip, gossip, gossip. It feels right, especially when your roommate is getting on your nerves, to start talking unkindly about him or her. But it's not right. Social isolation can be traumatizing, and it's just not fair to that person. Do the right thing and be direct. ▪

The Kleptomaniac

Steal—*intransitive verb*: to take the property of another wrongfully and especially as a habitual or regular practice.

Translation: If someone takes something that does not belong to him or her, that is stealing. If that person has asked ahead of time to use it and indicates he or she will return it, that is "borrowing." Big difference.

Some roommates assume it is all right to take something that does not belong to them because you share a room. One student told me how her roommate would always eat her food and then accuse her of never buying it. She even saw the same roommate sleeping with a quilt she knew was missing from a hall mate. It even had the hall mate's name embroidered on it, but the klepto just assumed it was all right for everyone on the floor to share.

If your belongings go missing, someone coming in and out of your room could be the culprit — be sure you know your facts before accusing your roommate of doing the stealing. The best solution is to set up guidelines when you first move in about using or borrowing personal items. It is easy for some people to confuse the two. Borrowing means you will use something and then give it back, but it should come with a request to do so. A roommate may "borrow" your hair conditioner, use some, and then put the bottle back. If you do not want this to happen, establish guidelines up front.

Is taking your laptop to the library because his does not work considered borrowing or stealing? Does the value of the item play into how you feel about this? To avoid these issues, you may want to think about various scenarios beforehand. If it is all right to borrow some things and not others, that can be a misleading message. You may want to consider setting a policy of "no borrowing," which means your roommate buys and uses his own stuff, and you do the same.

But let us say that never happened and your iPod is missing. Here are a few scenarios to help resolve this issue:

Scenario #1: You and your roommate did not draw up guidelines on borrowing or using each other's things. You walk in the room and see your iPod on your roommate's bed. He quickly removes the earphones and places the pillow over the iPod.

> "I noticed my iPod is missing. I always keep it in my backpack. Do you know where it is?"

> "I don't know what you're talking about."

> "I know that is my iPod. Please give it back to me. We should have had a conversation about borrowing each other's personal belongings, but we did not, so let us have one now." (State your position and let him do the same.)

Scenario #2: You and your roommate agreed before moving in that it was not all right to share personal items.

"I know you have my missing iPod. We agreed that it was not all right to share or borrow each other's personal things. I have held up my end of the agreement, and I expect you to do the same, so please do not take anything of mine again."

If the borrowing or stealing continues, tell your roommate you are reporting it to the RD. That may end the behavior, even if you do not tell the RD right away.

The Whiner

Here is some advice for when you become a parent: Tell your child he can cry, scream, or rant, but he cannot, under any circumstance, whine. There are few things as annoying as whining because those that do it never think in terms of solutions. In their world, **nothing is right and nothing will ever be right.** Every scenario, challenge, or situation is unfair. It is not even a matter of having things their way, but rather that they are victims and helpless to bring out the change that will end their whining.

CASE STUDY: THE WHINER

Melanie Falconer

I had to bring this story up as an example, even though it didn't take place in college. I had a friend from childhood who I invited up to visit me in my new city. I was feeling pretty lonely, especially because I moved and my boyfriend couldn't, so we had to do long distance. "Well, at least I'll get to see my best friend for a couple of days." I paid for half her plane ticket, spent a considerable amount on her Christmas gift, and hosted her during her stay.

Now, I'm not going to whine about it, because we did indeed have a great time laughing, eating some good food, and passing time with each other, but she really ended up not liking the city. Dare I say, she whined for the majority of the time. The weather was too cold. The "brick buildings were depressing," the river wasn't really "that pretty," and the food was "good" but not as good as the cheaper food in her town. The chai was "too spicy," while the other chai was "too sweet." When I was gone, I was gone for "too long," and the trains didn't wait "long enough" for people to board. She didn't understand what people liked about my new town, even though she knew I moved here to pursue becoming a copywriter while having a boy-friend who lived in another state.

The same friend whom I couldn't get enough of was driving me crazy. She wasn't even like this, who was she? I got resentful, of course, because I invested time, money, and energy in making sure she had a good visit even though I was pretty broke. This built up into resentment, and I told her up front a couple days after she left. It turned out she gets irritable in cold weather. She told me that no matter what, she usually just gets cranky if the temperature is below a certain level.

This didn't really excuse her behavior, especially given how much I was doing for her, but it did lead me to a discovery. What I discovered is that a "whiner" usually isn't a "whiner" all the time: there are certain situations or random things that will flip the switch for them, causing them to dwell on every little thing. If you're rooming with someone who is a whiner, it could be that she was forced to go to college by her parents, and she's fundamentally just not happy there. Whatever the scenario is, it usually isn't something you can control, and you shouldn't try to please everyone. It's more energy than it's worth.

In your post-college life, you will eventually be in a position to weed out the negative people in your life (unless you are related, which becomes more challenging). If a friend complains or whines about everything and anything, it brings negativity into your relationship and, therefore, into your life. If you have a whiner for a colleague, it is a little more difficult to remedy that situation, but you can distance yourself from that person socially. Also, if a colleague is a whiner, other people will be affected as well, and there is a better chance that someone else, such as a supervisor, will have to deal with him.

Some people can find fault and negativity in just about any situation. You can try to take control of a conversation with a whiner by asking specific questions or interrupting. Asking him or her to clarify his or her complaint gives the whiner a sense that you are interested in what he or she has to say. You may get to a point in which you have to say, "Well, there does not seem to be any solution that will please you," or, "I don't think any suggestion from me right now will help you solve this problem." It takes effort on your part to try to help a whiner come to a solution or see that there is a way out of what seems to him or her to be a no-win situation.

The Aggressor

If you watch reality television, you'll notice there is always one girl in particular who's "the aggressor." When things do not go her way, she acts out and retaliates against anyone she believes has betrayed her. She walks down the hall outside the girls' bedrooms and bangs two aluminum baking trays together while yelling for everyone to get up at 5 a.m. In another episode, she starts a hitting match with two girls and threw pillows and a tantrum. The girls have three reactions: laugh at her behavior and walk away, react in the same manner, or try to reason with her. This is not a woman open to discussion and negotiation. She acts and reacts purely based on her emotional state at the moment.

This is probably how you want your college experience to go, right?

Aggressiveness is probably the most off-putting trait a person can possess. It's probably more difficult to deal with than any of the traits we've discussed in this chapter because it's scary and ultimately comes off as anti-social. What's weird is that while the aggressor is sending the message "Don't mess with me!" he actually needs more love than anyone else. He probably possesses some similar traits as the "whiner," but instead of "whining," he rants, yells, and carries himself aggressively. The best thing to do is not engage him at their level of intensity. Be the straight man. Use the following strategies if you end up with a roommate who's an aggressor:

Wait for aggressor to stop talking (or yelling), and then ask, "Do you have anything else you want to say?" This indicates you're ready to change the subject.

- If the aggressor starts up again, be persistent in trying to put a stop to her behavior: "All right. I understand you're going through a lot, but I wish you would stop yelling."

Repeat the aggressor's name to try to turn her focus away from what she is saying to you.

Reiterate what you think the message is they are trying to convey, combining it with the strategy of saying their name:

"You're accusing me of using your hair products. That's not true,
_____."

"If you can stop for a minute, _____, I want to tell you my side
of the story."

- If the aggressor interrupts, repeat that you will only listen to what she
has to say when she is not yelling or pointing a finger in your face.

Tell them they need another source for expressing their anger because it's
too much for you. Suggest that they vent to a counselor, the RD, or even
join a debate club. Anger is a useful tool when it's in the right place, but
a dorm room is not one of them.

If their level of aggressiveness increases or you see that you cannot take
control of the situation, walk away without saying anything or say, "I'll
come back when you're calmer, and then we can talk." You do not have
to take verbal abuse from your roommate and if her aggressive behavior
continues to a point that it is effecting your living situation, go to your
RD or RA. You're paying to live there, and you don't need the extra stress
that could detract from the reason you came to college: to learn.

Adjusting Your Attitude

There are aspects of everyone's personality that will annoy another person.
If you are rooming with an opposite personality type, whether it is *the slob,
the whiner, the aggressor, the gossip, the slacker,* or, *the animal,* looking for
commonalities rather than differences may help reduce tension and conflict. Perhaps you like the same foods or music, or you both shop at the
same favorite clothing store. Discovering common ground can open the
door to a new facet of your relationship. It can also bring you closer to
your roommate and open the door to a conversation about personality
differences.

If you try to resolve a conflicting situation with your roommate and he does not immediately respond, try not to take it personally. He may be unaware there was a problem or embarrassed and unsure how to respond, especially if you caught him off guard. Also, the adage that there are two sides to every story is true (usually, there are many more). Your personality, habits, and behaviors may get on your roommate's nerves, and the roles may reverse with you being confronted rather than the other way around. Take heed of what your roommate has to say. Do not get on the offensive, but rather listen to what he has to say, do some self-reflection and see if there is truth to the matter. You can learn about yourself and your perception of other people when you are the one being confronted. It may be a hard lesson, but you are there to learn, right? In college, you learn just as much about yourself as, if not more than, the world around you.

Chapter 5

Cultural and Social Differences

Before you open your mouth and criticize Catholics, Jews, gays, minorities, liberals, or Republicans, think twice. Do not assume your roommate shares your point of view on anything religious, cultural, political, or ethical. Unless you have had these conversations with your roommate, you have no idea of his or her views and could offend your roommate and his or her family. It's not even about political correctness: freedom of speech demands that you take responsibility for what you say *especially* if it's disrespectful. Part of this responsibility is to understand the cultural and social differences that put a partition between you and your roommate (no, not the one you bought from Bed, Bath & Beyond).

Cultures are defined by many things: music, religion, place of birth, politics, clothes, food, and friends. Depending on where you attend college, you will either meet students from diverse cultural backgrounds or that population will be the smallest minority. While most large, urban institutions are the likeliest to house students from many different cultures, smaller, private colleges could be just as diverse. The size of the university matters less than geographic location and degree programs. A Catholic university may have a racially diverse student population, but you may not find many Jewish or Muslim people there. Even though historically black colleges enroll students of other races, the majority of students will be African-American. At urban universities or universities with a large number of graduate programs, you are likely to meet international students and students from culturally diverse backgrounds.

There are other behaviors related to social factors, such as one's gender, economic background, family upbringing, life experiences, and more that make a person different from you in significant and vital ways. If you are a man raised around other men who constantly sexualize and degrade women and continue this behavior in college, you will very likely outrage at least one woman at your university who will vocalize her opinion. If you lived in a family who never had to be concerned about money, tread carefully if you're used to wearing flashy clothes and always having the latest and greatest. The university experience is about ideas, not about stuff. Where some people might have thought that was cool in high school, some people at college may resent you or flat out ignore you if you keep talking about the new stuff you want to buy instead of Plato's *Dialogues*.

In sum, there is an endless list of things that can set you apart from another person. Differences can cause unintended miscommunication, conflict, tension, and hurt feelings. Even within the boundaries of the United States, people have different accents, cuisines, religions, values, and belief systems. Ironically, a person who grew up in the Midwest might have more in common with someone who grew up in New Zealand than in New York. You basically can never tell, but you *can* get smart and attuned to these differences so that no conflict will arise because of them.

Not All Cultures Think, Look, and Sound Alike

If you will be rooming with a foreign student or a student from a different background than yourself, that initial conversation (see "That First Conversation") is a good time to get to know more about his or her culture. This is the time to ask about where he or she grew up, when and why his or her family came to the United States, and what he or she likes or dislikes about living here versus his or her home country. Do not get carried away with too many questions or ask anything of a personal nature because you could mistakenly offend your roommate or it could sound as if you are interviewing him or her. You want to engage him or her in conversation but not overwhelm your roommate, so offer information about yourself and your family as well. Believe it or not, not every culture openly discusses personal experiences like Americans do so readily. Americans are notoriously direct, and can come off as abrasive to cultures that prefer indirect methods of communication. If your gut tells you he or she is not ready to answer some questions, hold off until you can get to know him or her face to face.

Students may also come to college with preconceived notions and stereotypes of people from other countries. They may have picked up those from home, school, the area in which they grew up, or through what they have read. Americans may perceive all Asian Americans as high academic achievers by nature of their ethnicity when it really has more to do with family values, whether their parents immigrated, and the pertinent role of education in child-rearing within that culture. There is no better environment than higher education to learn about and dispel stereotypes as you will meet students from worlds and cultures quite different from yours. You might even be inspired to take a class on the history and cultures of other countries.

There are behaviors that we (Americans) do not think twice about that are offensive to those of another culture, such as personal space (Americans tend to require more "personal space" than other cultures), too much eye contact, and a more liberal form of dress. There are also differences Americans may find offensive such as hygiene, what other cultures deem appropriate for discussion, and more. These differences are minor compared to overarching cultural norms and beliefs, and the best way to navigate them is to simply look up information on their culture's social etiquette.

A Word for the Wise...

If you room with someone from a different cultural background, do so. It can be a rewarding learning experience for both of you, even if you encounter some barriers.

Bigotry and Racism

College is a place where you may encounter people of different races and backgrounds more often than you ever have before.

It is possible that you will be tempted to make judgments about people based on their race or the color of their skin rather than treating them as unique individuals. This temptation is understandable, especially if you are encountering people with backgrounds that you have never seen before, but you should realize that making assumptions about them because of their race is wrong and refuse to let your speech and actions reflect those assumptions.

Language that is racially divisive may damage your chances of making connections and relationships at college. People of one color might think it is all right to make a racially charged remark in front of other people who share their race. Before making those comments, look around, especially if you are at a large urban university. There are students of all colors and racial backgrounds, and one of them might end up being your best friend—but maybe not if you say hurtful things that belittle or unfairly generalize about that person's race or ethnicity.

The university or college may also have guidelines on how to treat your fellow students, and you may get in trouble if you make remarks or commit actions that are not in accordance with university policy.

It may be hard at times to know if a remark is offensive, and people may disagree if it is. For instance, some people think that Popeyes recently asking Jerry Rice to advertise their fried chicken wrongly perpetuates a racist stereotype of African-Americans loving fried chicken. Others see it as racist to criticize a man for advertising chicken simply because he is black.

Because college is a melting pot of different opinions, values, lifestyles, and beliefs, someone may call you out for being racist when you did not intend to disrespect anyone. How can you tell if you're being racist—and if you are, why should you stop being so?

Racism and bigotry are morally wrong. Everyone is an individual and should be judged on his or her individual weaknesses and strengths, not by his or her biologically ordained appearance. It would be a lie to say that these aren't problems for us anymore. But focusing on external features more than humanity is never right—no one wants to be put in a box (for instance, don't assume that Asians love math), and no one wants to be treated with disrespect (for instance, don't use racist epithets that have derogatory meanings).

If, on the other hand, you have a roommate who continuously makes remarks that are offensive, either to your cultural background or someone else's, let him know immediately:

"You know, when you make those kinds of comments, you are offending not only me, but an entire population of people. Unless you go to the Census Bureau, gather up everyone to which your comments would apply in one huge auditorium, and say them shamelessly in front of all of them, then don't say them."

"Freedom of speech means I also have the right to say what I think: Your comments are unnecessarily hateful and unfounded in logic."

"When you say those things, you are insulting me and my family. I'm sure you wouldn't like it if someone insulted your family."

"I don't know where you're getting some of your ideas about my culture, but you're way off base. If you're interested in the truth, I'd be happy to share with you."

Meanwhile, Back at the Dorm . . .

So, you have some dorm-mates with bigoted attitudes or beliefs? Are they sexist? Classist, even? Bigotry and prejudices don't have to do with just race. Perhaps the most frightening aspect of prejudices is that we can have them and not even know it. If someone in your dorm or a group of people are making comments that make you uncomfortable, you have every right to express your discomfort. If you find that these people take up the majority of your dorm, it might be more energy than it's worth; request to change halls and call it a day. ∎

Differences in Sexuality

Some straight students have no problem rooming with someone who is openly gay. Others will encounter a gay peer for the first time in their lives (even though they may have known people who had not yet come out).

College is when many young people experiment with sexuality. For some, it is part of learning, getting to know yourself and coming to terms with who you are.

For some students who have gay friends or family members, rooming with a gay student is not a big deal. They can get on your nerves as much as a straight roommate, and you will encounter conflict over issues that have nothing to do with sexual preference. For those who may not be as comfortable in this situation, there are some concerns, questions, and fears that may arise:

- If I'm rooming with a gay student, will people who are just getting to know me think I am gay too?

- Is there a chance he or she will become attracted to me because we live together?

- What if my gay roommate has someone spend the night? That will make me twice as uncomfortable.

- What will my parents think?

- I am religiously opposed to homosexuality.

All of these are valid concerns, but some may be easier to deal with than you think.

For instance, the best way to "laugh off" accusations from other people that because your roommate is gay, you must be gay, is to do just that: laugh it off. You could just shrug and say something like this:

"Well, I happen to not be gay."

Simple. See how easy that was? The more you try to explain, the more it will appear as if you have something to defend.

It may be more difficult to handle talking to your parents about it, but this too can be managed. If you think your parents will be uncomfortable visiting because, for example, your father bad mouths homosexuals, and you like your roommate and do not want her to be embarrassed, you should warn your roommate ahead of time. with the caveat that it is your father's viewpoint — not yours. You and she may want to make arrangements when she will not be in the room, to avoid a tense situation for everyone.

Arrangements for romantic partners spending the night don't have to be that much different than for two straight roommates — courtesy and respect for the other person's needs and right to the living space should prevail.

If you are uncomfortable due to religious or moral beliefs, realize that just like you may disagree with your roommate's perspective on other issues, such as politics, religion, lifestyle, and friends,you still have to treat your roommate with respect. Even if you have no problem with homosexuality, you may not want to live in the same space as someone with a sexuality different from your own. Don't shun your roommate or leave him in the lurch. It may not be possible for you to switch roommates freshman year. If you would rather not room with someone who is gay in the future, that's fine — and if it is necessary to switch freshman year, try your best to make sure that this is a mutual solution (for instance, your roommate may want to have a roommate who fully supports his sexual choices, and so you may be able to agree that it's best to part ways as roommates).

Here are a couple of skills and strategies to deal with a different sexuality:

Ask Them.

America is famous for its divides. We think in black and white, with no grayscale in between. Part of the reason why a rainbow is fitting as a symbol for homosexuality is that sexuality exists on a spectrum. A person who is "straight" may not be just "straight" but have moments where he or she is attracted to a person of the same sex, or even desires to *be* another sex. Believe it or not, I have a friend who has no sexuality at all! But in America, we tend to keep it in extremes: you're straight, or you're gay.

In reality, you shouldn't be so uncomfortable with people who have a different sexuality than your own. That's only one part of them, and if you're curious about it, and how it's shaped their life, you should ask them! Think of getting to know them like visiting another country: you don't have to adopt their attitudes or beliefs, but you can be curious about them.

Observe them.

For some people, their sexuality doesn't define them as much as other things do. I remember seeing an incredibly handsome man walk into my Spanish class. He was the spitting image of Brandon Flowers. I sat next to him almost every class; we laughed and got to know each other in an incredibly romantic language. He was incredibly interested in Spanish culture, linguistics, science, and music. I swear, the day I was going to ask him out was the day he told me he was gay!

To him, it was just a casual fact of life. He liked men and didn't talk about it much.

Now, for others, their sexuality is an emblem of pride. Many people have been fighting for the right to be treated the same as people who are straight, so for some their sexuality is a rallying call. They have every right to be proud and express their opinion.

Maybe for some reason, this makes you uncomfortable. If it does, it's okay to express your discomfort. Just say you have a relatively conservative attitude, and don't enjoy discussing sexuality as openly as they might.

A Word for the Wise . . .

There will be situations in which roommates cannot live together because of opposing lifestyles and resulting conflicts that cannot be resolved. Sexuality is a part of one's identity that can't be changed, but it is also a way of life. There are even significant differences between straight people: one person may be more sexually active than the other. These differences can cause tension, and if it is too much, it might be best to request to move in with another dorm-mate.

You're a What?

You may ask why a section on this topic even needs to be included in this book. It is a relatively new area that is being addressed on campuses across the nation, while it has yet to be heard of at others. However, as with much of this book, the information in this section is designed to prepare you for circumstances you may encounter as a college resident.

"Trans" and "gender-nonconforming student" are terms you should become familiar with — they are receiving more national and media attention as more students go public with their stories.

A trans student is one who is born as a male or female, but has decided to live life, including that at college, as the opposite gender. A transmale is a woman who lives life as a male, but is still technically a woman. He may have a girlfriend, he may receive testosterone shots, have corrective surgery, and legally change his name, but he may choose to attend a women's college,. Typically, they are places that foster progressive thinking when it comes to gender roles and would be considered a safer environment for the trans student: there is usually no additional physical threat to students and the trans student may have more in common with female students. Colleges at which trans students have a presence have created transgender or gender-neutral bathrooms, changing rooms, and locker rooms. Terminology to raise awareness of this student population includes:

- transgender
- transmale(s) or transmen
- trans person
- trans people
- trans activist
- trans organization
- trans identity

- trans students

- trans community

You may be scratching your head, trying to figure out what this has to do with you. Well, let us say you are a female student and are assigned to a trans student roommate—someone who was born as a female, but lives life as male. The question is whether you are rooming with a male or female student.

According to Campus Pride, "998 colleges and universities have nondiscrimination policies that include gender identity/expression." But even that doesn't mean that the university or college will be a good fit. Several years ago, a feature story in *The New York Times Magazine* included one example of a transmale student who enrolled at a private women's college. His roommates complained to the RA about being asked to share a room with a man. The student told his roommates on the first day that he was a trans, but the women were troubled by this on several levels: they were attending a women's college to learn and live in a single-gender environment, and they felt uncomfortable referring to him by male pronouns. This person ended up transferring to another college, and other students in this situation found themselves isolated, unless their university has a trans organization in which they can become involved and meet students with similar issues.

If you are assigned to a transgender roommate and it makes you uncomfortable, you should take it up with your RD and discuss ways to approach whatever issues you're having.

A Word for the Wise . . .

Throughout your college years, you will encounter students who have cho-sen non-traditional life styles. Part of a college experience is to meet new people, make new friends, and learn about life choices that are different from your own. You shouldn't shy away from situations that make you uncomfortable because the university is (ideally) a tolerant place. Maybe they're not the problem, and you need to open up your mind.

Raising Awareness

College is a place to explore new ideas, forge new friendships, and discover cultures, communities, and ideologies that make up a well-rounded educa-tion. You will have the opportunity to interact with people from walks of life similar and quite different from yours. This isn't restricted to what was covered in this chapter alone: economic background, values, religion, atti-tudes towards gender, and more can make you incredibly different from another person.

If you are looking for a particular experience, the *U.S. News and World Report's America's Best Colleges* is a good place to start, with lists and profiles of those universities and colleges. For example, if you are gay, you would likely want to steer away from conservative religious schools and instead look for those that have previously established clubs and support groups for gay, lesbian, bisexual, and transgender students. If a cross-cultural cur-riculum is important to you, look for schools that offer coursework in global issues, gender roles, world religions, social activism, and programs abroad. Those are also the schools that are more likely to offer extracurric-ular opportunities and organizations that mirror those academic areas.

While it's incredibly important to stay open throughout your entire college experience, you don't want to be uncomfortable the entire time. Seek out colleges where you know you'll get the support you need.

Chapter 6

Conflict Management and Serious Issues

Conflict is inevitable. In an ideal world, everyone in college would get his or her own room and not have to share a private space with anyone—or at least anyone he or she didn't like. But in a shared room situation, privacy is a luxury. You will get to know a person in a way that you won't get to know anyone else in college. You will have many times where you and that person will be in the same room for hours, either doing your nightly routine, relaxing, or studying. This book isn't meant to scare you: in reality, a lot of living situations have a funny way of working themselves out, bettering you and your roommate, and teaching you both critical life skills such as tolerance, patience, cooperation, and respect. But even in very positive roommate relationships, conflict of some kind is bound to happen at some point.

Then, of course, there are *serious* issues. Not issues arising from a difference in personality, lifestyle, or beliefs, but psychological issues a person may have and need to work through. Unfortunately, they tend to become exacerbated when people start college, since it can be one of the most stressful transitions (note: transitions, not "period") of young adulthood. You're away from your family for the first time, your studies are intense, there are large stretches of unstructured time, and you may be in a completely different city than what you're used to. So it's not surprising that this is when serious mental issues may begin or begin to get worse than they already are.

The most important thing to do is to be able to distinguish from "small character defect" to "serious mental disorder," which the following sections will help you to do. This chapter is dedicated to giving your strategies to deal with conflicts, big and small, and also explains how to detect and confront serious issues.

Conflict or Friendly Disagreement?

There are classic cases of people in and out of public eye who are in successful relationships but disagree on fundamental issues, be they political or religious. California Governor Arnold Schwarzenegger is a lifelong Republican while his wife, Maria Shriver, is not only a Democrat, but comes from one of the most highly visible line of Democrats in the country's history: the Kennedy family. Political pundits James Carville (Democrat) and Mary Matalin (conservative Republican) are married and appear regularly on the TV circuit. Even the Sunday morning political roundtable members offer opposite points of view but are clearly sometimes enjoying each other's company and are friends off the set. In these examples, the conflicts have little to do with each other's personalities but more so the issues for which each person feels strongly about.

If you think you have encountered a conflict with your roommate, try to separate the issue from the personality. Ask yourself if the conflict has to do with the way your roommate is behaving, including habits you may find annoying, or if it is an inherent personality trait, such as whining or gossiping. Think about your desired outcome and how you can bring that about. Attacking someone's personality versus asking him or her to correct a behavior will make a difference in whether your desired outcome is achieved.

When you do not see eye to eye with your roommate, it is all right to agree to disagree. You may not agree with his viewpoint or opinion, but part of being an adult is to accept and respect different points of view, especially if you value the relationship. It's okay to discuss these viewpoints, since it is college after all, but don't let it escalate into an intense debate if you think it will leave residual tension between you and your roommate. If your roommate has a belief that he or she doesn't want to change, don't try to change it.

Take the following story.

Pete and Rob got along great. They joined the same fraternity their first year on campus and hung out with a group of friends they met through Habitat for Humanity. But Rob considered Pete to be a slob. Rob was not obsessed with cleanliness but liked order in their small dorm room and was constantly calling Pete a "pig" or a "slob":

> "Pete. You're a pig," Rob would say.

Is it Pete's personality that is causing the conflict over cleanliness, or is it a behavior that's not fundamental to who he is? In other words, is it correctable or an inherent component of who Pete is?

Calling Pete a name is going to have little impact on whether he is willing to correct his behavior, as it is a personal attack. By calling Pete a pig, Rob is attacking Pete, not the problem behavior. Explaining to Pete why his behavior is annoying and why he should correct it (the desired outcome) is more likely to bring about change:

> "Pete, you're a great guy, but I'm used to living in a tidier setting. It's stressful living in this much mess. Could you make an effort to tidy up at least once a week?"

Here there is no name calling, and Rob is asking him to correct his behavior and explaining why using an "I" statement. This approach lets Pete know that his behavior has a direct effect on Rob.

Behaviors that are in one's control tend to follow along the lines of cleanliness, communication, scheduling, personal hygiene, and noise level. While we all have our distinct preferences, these things can be changed to suit the needs and comfort level of your roommate. There are things that usually can't be, and shouldn't really be, changed about a person, such as his or her gender, race, sexuality, religion, interests, sense of morals, mannerisms, ways of expressing himself or herself, and other things that tend to develop early on in childhood and young adulthood. If you are agreeable with these things that make a person *who he or she is* but disagree with their habits, then you have every right to discuss the matter.

The Beginnings and Building of Conflict

When tension builds between people due to a conflict, the recipient of the door slams, silence, and dirty looks is not always aware of the problem. If you are suddenly the recipient of the "cold shoulder" treatment from your roommate, try to get her to verbalize what is going on. You probably do not want to ask outright if she is angry with you as that implies there may be a reason. She may be having a problem with a relationship, classes, or her family, so there is a chance it has nothing to do with you. But if you find her behavior is directly affecting your comfort level with her, it is best not to ignore it. You may try this approach:

"I noticed you have been quiet lately. Is something going on?"

This opens the door for her to share or respond directly if the reason for a tense environment has to do with you. If the response is, "I do not want to talk about it," the reason is either private or because the situation is about your relationship and she does not want to address it. A good response from you would be:

"All right. If you do want to talk at some point, I am here to listen."

But if the tension gets worse and does not go away, you will end up feeling angry and resentful. Living in a tense environment, whether it is in a romantic or family relationship, is never healthy for anyone. At that point, you should address the problem with your RD, tell him or her what's going on and get some outside intervention. Sometimes, an outside mediator is necessary to solve the problem, though you don't want to rely on it (you won't have this resource as an adult).

If you're the one with a complaint about or gripe with your roommate, verbalize it before your anger builds and the tension increases to an intolerable level. The longer you wait to address conflict, the more difficult it becomes to address it. However, never try to address conflict in a state of heightened emotion. (This is also advice to carry over into personal relationships.) There is a higher chance that you, or the other person, will say something hurtful that cannot be taken back with an apology.

Also, beware of the "anger explosion" that can occur when certain people have narcissistic personality traits. These people can be particularly difficult to deal with in terms of conflict management. Most everyone knows someone with this personality trait. He or she seems laid back and easygoing but something is eating away at him or her. When his or her anger over the situation builds and builds, he or she goes off on a tirade and issues or conflicts that come from his or her past: This is the "explosion." That behavior leaves the other person in a no-win situation. Basically, the conversation ceased to be about the two of them.

Keep returning to how that person is impacting *you*. Make your feelings known, and remind him or her that there are consequences for what he or she says and does.

Strategies for Listening and Responding

To be an active listener, show with your body, facial expression, and verbal response that you hear what he or she is saying. You can nod your head on occasion or say "yes" or "uhmmm hmmm" to show that you acknowledge and empathize about what he or she is saying, even if the other person is ranting and saying things that are untrue. Addressing the person by name will also show her that you are in the moment and aware of her emotional state. The tone and volume of your voice are important as well. One tactic to quell a rant from your roommate is to repeat what she is saying, using "I" and "you" along with rephrasing her words.

For example, say your roommate has been having problems with her family. In the same week, she failed two exams and knows if she does not pick up her grades, she will lose her scholarship. She is angry with herself and her family. She left the door unlocked, and when you came back from class, it was wide open. Luckily, nothing was missing, but this is not the first time you had to remind her to lock up.

You: When I came back from class, the door was unlocked and wide open. *(You are stating a fact and your point of view without anger or accusation.)*

Roommate: You criticize everything I do. No matter what I do, it is just not good enough for you. I think I want to move out.

You: Okay . . . *(You are acknowledging, but not agreeing, to what she is saying.)*

Roommate: Didn't you hear what I said? You are not even listening to me. You never listen to what I have to say.

You: I am listening, Emily. Go ahead and say what you need to say.

(You are affirming that you hear her. You address her by name)

You let her rant for a while and she calms down. There is some silence.

You: I understand it has been a tough week for you. <u>You</u> are saying that <u>I</u> criticize everything you do, but both of us know that is not true. <u>I</u> realize that you are upset right now and may not realize what you are saying.

(You are using "you" and "I" to personalize the situation. You let her know you are empathetic to her dilemma, but you have also stated your point of view—that she left the door unlocked and that is unacceptable behavior.)

Another useful tactic to detract a rant is to address the person by name and to ask questions to help your roommate regain focus. We have all been emotional at times and will ramble, repeat ourselves, and not make sense. Some emotional outbursts happen even when one has planned out what he or she is going to say. In a situation of heightened emotions, another person's reaction can trigger an outburst and unreasonable behavior. If you have ever watched the television show *Intervention* family and friends confront a loved one with a preconceived list of what they want to say. Even with best intentions, the response of their loved one will throw them off track, causing them to cry, not be able to follow through, and their loved one becoming verbally caustic or storming out of the room.

By combining a few tactics, you not only gather additional information about what the other person is saying, but you help him or her to focus on his or her words, no matter how unreasonable. Here are some strategies for how to do this:

- Addressing the person by name

- Asking specific questions to gather more information

- Stating your point of view or position in a calm manner

- Using "I" and "you" language, focusing on behaviors and feelings

- Avoid using labels ("You're such a whiner!")

- Use your reasoning instead of your emotions

CASE STUDY: LIVING WITH A STRANGER

Kylie Widseth
University of Florida

Going to school over a thousand miles away from your Nebraska home definitely isn't something that a typical person would do. So right out of the gate, I was already a weird one. And going to school at the University of Florida, I was already heavily stereotyped. Do you live on a farm? Do you eat corn every day? Do you drive your tractor to school? I can answer all of those questions with a definite and solid *no*. Are there parts of the state where this may be true? Of course, but I lived in the city. There is a major difference between city folk and country folk, and that was hard for a lot of people to understand. Also, that carbonated beverage is definitely pop, not soda.

Each graduating class had a group page on Facebook, so I immediately joined my class page when I was accepted into UF. I noticed that everyone was posting bios about themselves, and I was desperate to find a roommate because I was already the odd ball out. I noticed a lot of people were saying that they wanted an out-of-state roommate. I was eager to find someone to live with, so I jumped at the chance. After messaging back and forth with a few girls, my roommate and I decided that we wanted to live together.

We ended up exchanging numbers, and we talked a lot about our lives and how we wanted to decorate the dorm. We were both very excited to finally be out of high school and experience the freedom of college.

After weighing a bunch of options of where to live, we had decided to live in Riker Hall, a one-bedroom dorm with two single beds and a communal bathroom. Riker Hall was where her sister had lived, and it was close to a lot of the sports facilities. We both really wanted to attend sporting events, so we chose a place that was pretty central to both our classes and where all the sports teams played.

After talking a lot over the summer, I felt like I really knew her. I would talk to her about my occasional dramas, and I vented to her sometimes. I also followed her on Facebook and Twitter, and I enjoyed seeing posts about her life. Twitter wasn't a social media platform I used very often, and I think she must have known that. I would occasionally go on Twitter and see a tweet and think *hey, that kind of sounds like she is talking about me*, and she definitely was. I can't prove it, but sometimes, you just kind of know. The things she said were never good either; it was always something bad about me, and it was usually referring to something I vented to her about. As you can imagine, I was kind of upset about it, but after awhile, I just let it go.

The first week or so, our RA (resident assistant) sat down with my roommate and I and made a sort of contract with us. We had to agree on things like how we could keep our room (messy, clean, or in between), how late we would stay up, who would take the trash out, if we would allow guests over, what temperature we would keep the room, etc. We agreed we would keep our room relatively clean. I kept my side in pristine condition, while she was incredibly messy. I wasn't even upset that she would be messy — I was honestly more upset that she lied about being cleaner.

I knew that my roommate was very smart, so I had just naturally assumed that she would probably need to study as much as I did. I imagined our dorm room to be pretty quiet on any given day. Often, while I was studying, she would be watching Netflix or YouTube videos, which was fine. But she was also known for having a very loud laugh, which would scare me while I was studying. To be clear, I realize that some people have to try harder at school than others. I would mainly get frustrated that she would get good grades without studying, while I would study for hours and get the same grades, if not worse grades. I knew her studying habits, because there weren't any.

But honestly, I wouldn't even say my roommate experience was bad. I would say it was pretty average overall. Every time I would tell my parents about my annoyances with her, they would always say, "Well, it could be worse." I totally agree, and I was always grateful that my experience was average and not terrible. I had heard horror stories about other people's roommates.

But there was at least one good thing that happened my freshman year — I met the girl who I would live with for the remainder of my college career. I didn't know it at the time, but on the first day of school, she actually stalked me on Facebook and figured out that we were in a lot of the same classes. I remember reading her Facebook message saying she lived next door. She would explain the story differently, but it was a little creepy nonetheless. From that single message, we became best friends.

So there really is a silver living to every situation. And maybe, just maybe, message or talk to that person on your floor who you know is taking the same classes as you, because you never know where it may lead.

Conflict Resolution Primer

The most effective remedy for conflict is communication. When countries are at a hostile standoff, talks among leaders are encouraged. When a marriage breaks down, couples seek talk therapy to open the lines of communication. Even on elementary school playgrounds, where conflict is a daily issue, the resolution entails communication between teachers, students, and then the students to each other.

You might be asking yourself if learning these communication skills is even necessary. Isn't it possible to completely avoid conflict with your roommate(s) throughout your college career? Not really. When I asked roommates if they ever had an argument, the answer was always "yes." When I asked if there was ever tension or if they ever got on each other's nerves, again, the answer was "yes." Did these minor glitches get in the way of these roommates getting along and surviving in the same space for the duration of the school year? Sometimes yes and most of the time no.

However, let us assume, in the spirit of being prepared, that you will encounter a major conflict with your roommate.

If you have taken the time to get to know your roommate, including his habits, likes and dislikes, schedule, and cultural and family background, you will have a better sense of who he is, which will help you implement these general strategies before conflict begins to boil:

- *Figure out what's in your control.* Is there something you can do to work around the differences without even saying anything to your room-mate? Are there times when you can be outside of the room to give yourself some space? Are you being too critical or controlling and just need to let go?

- *Discuss differences with your roommate.* There is such a thing as being *too* optimistic: it's called being in denial. If there's something you abso-lutely know is going to bother you, discuss it with them. That way, if it becomes an issue, you can refer to your earlier discussion and come off as more credible.

- *Decide whether it's livable.* It surprisingly takes little time to decide whether you can really live with a person or not. When someone is out of control or seems mentally unstable, this is when it's not livable, and the solution to your problems is to simply talk with your RD about moving into a different dorm room. If a person is none of these things, then yes, you *can* learn (and should learn) how to live with him (at least for the first year).

Once a conflict does occur, there are several goals in planning a meeting to try to resolve conflicts. You want to respect everyone's point of view in the same way you want yours respected. You also want to come to some kind of an agreement. It may take several meetings to get there, but think of that as your ultimate goal. Eventually, you will need to come to an agreement on actions necessary to bring about change—and maybe you will need it to be signed rather than verbal.

Each person takes a turn stating his or her side to the story. This is the hard part: Try to state your side without demonstrating anger, without crying, without blame, and without malice. You will read this over and over in this section: Use "I" and "you" throughout. This is crucial in communicating the issues. State what the offense is. Also state how your roommate's action made you feel. State the reason that you think your roommate did whatever she did. Then state the resolution you'd like to see.

What was the offense? Your "you" statement:

You did _____. You said _____.

How did it make you feel? Your "I" statement:

I was _____ when you _____. I felt (angry, hurt, left out) _____ when you _____.

Why I believe you did or said that.

You must have been _____ when you did that.

You must have done that because you felt _____.

What resolution do you desire? What action needs to be taken to resolve conflict?

What I would like us to do is _____. What I need from you is _____.

Meanwhile, Back at the Dorm . . .

If you think you can avoid conflict entirely, you don't know what's coming. If you won't disagree with your roommate, you will surely disagree with a dorm-mate. The dorms could be co-ed with single gender floors, all one gender, or full of just incredibly different people. There will be plenty of opportunities to clash with the people in your dorm: in the bathrooms, the dining halls, the lounges, or community events. Even when groups start to form, make sure to deal with conflicts individually. Don't start confronting the problem in front of everyone: it will only make it that much worse. ■

How to Communicate the Problem

Controlling emotions when confronting the person with whom you have a conflict is the first step in successful resolution. Anyone who has argued with a friend or family member, which is most everyone, can recall the point when a confluence of emotions came together: pent-up anger, jealousy, mistrust. When this happens, things are said, accusations are made and reasoning is clouded by heightened emotions.

If you and your roommate come head-to-head over an issue, or several, there is bound to be an argument at some point, and what makes the "walking away" approach more difficult is that you can only do so temporarily; you both have to live in the same space. But walking away from roommate confrontation is all right if you have intentions of readdressing the problem. Take a break. Cool down and come back to try again. Take stock of what this relationship means to you. If you only see your roommate in passing because you are both busy, how much time and energy do you want to invest in resolving conflict? If you like your roommate but are just going through a rough patch, make the effort. Take a look at how you may be responsible for what is happening and do some soul searching of your own.

Maybe you have decided the relationship is worth salvaging. You want to resolve the conflict, but you are both angry and no one is talking. Now you have to come up with a way to communicate with your roommate in an effective, empathetic, and understanding way.

The only way to do this is *face to face*.

Email can convey words and conserve time, but it cannot convey verbal signals, which are key to successful and meaningful communication. Email also makes it easy to vent anger and frustration through the use of words, but unless you take a few moments and re-read what you wrote, or wait until the next day to see if your feelings have changed, once you press "send," there is no getting it back. Communicating by phone provides verbal signals that convey emotion and tone, but this communication method lacks eye contact.

Both methods cannot convey key signals that not only connect people in relationships, but are useful when confronting or resolving conflict: body language, eye contact, hand movement, and facial expression. Even the way you sit or stand during conversation, whether it is friendly or confrontational, tells the other person something about yourself and your feelings in addition to the words you use.

Today's college students instant message their friends about everything. It is not only a communication tool that defines their generation, but one well within their comfort level. Used to convey the most minute, personal information, it is no surprise that email or messaging is the delivery method most students will prefer to communicate a problem with their roommate. But going back with emails with tones of increasing anger and frustration still leaves an unsolved problem and even further creates a void of communication. Unless you are an exceptional communicator, you will not be able to resolve conflict through text messaging. You can perhaps come to some kind of temporary truce, such as, "All right. I'll never sit on your bed again," but the tone in that example alone insinuates a hidden message: "I'll do this now to make you shut up, but promise that I'll never sit on your bed again? Get real." The issues at the base of the conflict are still there—looming around the corner—only to be solved by an actual conversation.

Warning! When to Call in a Third Party

When attempts to resolve a conflict on your own have failed, it is time to involve an objective third party. If your first inclination is to bring in a mutual friend, that could result in a loss of friendship as your roommate will feel he is outnumbered and that the friend is siding with you. If you feel you have given your roommate the benefit of the doubt and have made valid attempts to calmly discuss the conflict and provide possible resolutions, and he still will not listen, let him know you have no other alternative but to tell the RD, but invite him to come as well. Make sure to do this *before* actually going to the RD. Usually, this can be a wake-up call enough to get your roommate to start making necessary changes.

An exception to this would be if you feel your safety is being compromised and the situation is an emergency. Then you should directly to the RD without feeling you need to first inform your roommate.

When you get to this point, explain the situation to the RD and be specific about how you have tried to resolve it on your own and what your roommate's response has been. In other words, operate at your highest level, stay reasoned and rational, and don't act like a kid telling on her brother or sister. What you do not want to do is demand action from the RD or threaten to bring in a higher-level authority, such as his or her supervisor. You will make a permanent enemy in doing so.

The RD will determine whether the problem is fixable. Let your RD know you want your roommate to be part of the discussion and stress your interest in resolving the conflict rather than saying you will just move into another dorm. In all honesty, moves during the first year are very uncommon. The administration expects you to learn as much as you can in your situation and then simply chose another roommate for next year.

Student counseling services may provide direct meditation or conflict resolution services to help you resolve conflict. To be proactive, attend a conflict resolution workshop. The RD, housing office, or counseling services can also give you feedback and advice on resolving conflict. These are trained professionals who deal with students with a myriad of problems, complaints, and issues, so take advantage of their expertise. There is no reason for you to reinvent the wheel and try to get through this on your own.

A Word for the Wise . . .

If you feel there is no other alternative but to take the problem to the resident staff, tell your roommate you are doing so and invite him or her to come along so both sides of the story are heard and you are not later accused of doing something behind his back.

Meanwhile, Back at the Dorm . . .

The RDs are usually people who are close to your age. Unfortunately, this can sometimes undermine their authority. Sometimes they'll become close with people in their dorm, though they are not really supposed to, and play favorites. Thankfully, they usually have two RDs to balance each other out, one male and one female. If you don't feel comfortable with your RDs, go to the housing office and explain why.

On another note, if you feel like you don't want to complain to your RD, that you want to stick it out with your roommate and be as positive as you can, then do it! Make sure to scope out potential roommates for next year in your dorm. ■

Substance Abuse and Your Roommate: What You Can Do

What action should you take if your roommate is abusing drugs or alcohol? First, assess whether your safety is being compromised. As a dorm resident, you may be held accountable for illegal activity taking place in your room, whether you have initiated it or not. If there is any kind of illegal drug activity taking place in your dorm room, be adamant with your roommate that you will not tolerate it and that you will report him or her to the RD if it happens again. If you need other advice, go to the counseling or student health center. Sessions are confidential so your name will not be attached to your inquiry. Let the counselor know you want to help your roommate get help.

Do not cover for your roommate or enable him to skip class, miss work, or lie to family and friends. It is likely he will deny he has a problem, instead trying to convince you it is only a weekend activity or that he can stop at any time. Use the same approach tactics as you would for a roommate with depression or an eating disorder: be sensitive but firm in your position. If there was a particular incident or a repeated behavior that frightened you or compromised your daily life, be honest. As always, encourage him to seek professional help:

> "I cannot take any more of you coming in at 3 a.m. and getting sick in the bathroom. It is not fair to me and I think you need to get help."

> "I found a needle in the bathroom trash. I want to give you a chance to tell me what's going on before I go to someone about this. Doing drugs in our room is unacceptable to me."

> "I was really scared the other night when you brought your friends home so late. You were all drunk, and I had to spend the night in a friend's room. This can't happen again."

If you are ever faced with the possibility that your roommate is suffering from a drug overdose, the signs to look for include: slurred speech, obvious lack of coordination, abnormal breathing, slow or rapid pulse, big or small pupils, heavy sweating, hallucinations, and, unconsciousness.

Do not be afraid to call for help. You may be worried you will get your friend in trouble, or if you have been using, you will as well. But by not doing something, there is a real threat to this person's life. A drug overdose can, and often does, result in severe physical consequences.

Call campus security or 911 for an ambulance. Another good number to have around is the Poison Control Center at **1-800-222-1222**. You will be automatically connected to the center nearest you. Better safe than sorry.

College Students and Mental Health Issues

One hears that college represents some of the best years of our lives. While college provides an ideal setting for intellectual and personal growth, it can be overwhelming for the average student but even more so for those with existing mental health issues.

The causes of mental illness within college student populations may result from unresolved childhood issues, the stress of adjusting to a new life away from home, transitioning from childhood to adulthood, ending or beginning a romantic relationship, family issues, or having difficulty coming to terms with national tragedies (September 11 or Virginia Tech shootings, for example). The most common mental health issues experienced by college students in the 21st century include:

- Depression

- Anxiety disorders

- Self injury

- Eating disorders

According to college counseling centers, more students are arriving on campus with a range of mental health problems and high stress levels. Some college counseling centers are struggling with higher demands of students seeking services. A 2012 survey completed by the Association for University and College Counseling Center Directors states that "95 percent of college counseling center directors said the number of students with significant psychological problems is a growing concern in their center or on campus." The survey also expected this number to only grow in the coming years.

Colleges and universities are stepping up to the plate to address the increased demand for services by hiring additional counselors to reduce the wait time for an appointment. To reduce the stigma associated with seeking counseling, more universities and colleges are implementing outreach and peer-to-peer groups, and providing training sessions for all students on how to recognize signs of mental illness. Many also offer free counseling sessions or ensuring that visits are covered under the university's student health insurance program.

It is advised that if a pre-college student has existing mental health issues that will require ongoing treatment, he or she, along with his or her parents, should investigate the university's services beforehand. Check the website to find out the fee schedule and the number of counselors on the staff.

A Word for the Wise . . .

If you are serious about trying to help your roommate suffering from a form of mental illness, first educate yourself to recognize the symptoms. Seek help through the university's counseling or student health offices. Do not try to help when uninformed.

Depression

Symptoms of depression include sadness; anxiety; decreased energy or fatigue; loss of interest or pleasure in usual activities; sleep disturbances; appetite and weight changes; feelings of hopelessness, guilt, and worthlessness; thoughts of death or suicide, or suicide attempts; difficulty concentrating, making decisions, or remembering; irritability or excessive crying; and chronic aches and pains not explained by another physical condition. Stressful events or major lifestyle changes such as divorce, death of a loved one or serious illness can trigger episodes of depression.

Depression is a little too difficult to spot, as some people have "depressed personalities." They say some of the greatest philosophers were depressed, because they had an acute sense of reality. But there is a difference between being mildly depressed and a sort of cynical person by nature and being depressed to the point that it prevents you from taking care of yourself. If you notice yourself slipping away, unable to feel motivated, go to class, and take care of basic things due to a depressed state of mind, this is the time to do something. Likewise if you see your roommate in a similar state.

In addition to the resources students can find within the university's counseling and student health centers, many are educating housing staff on recognizing the signs of depression to help guide students toward treatment. If you see your roommate with signs of debilitating depression, you can express your concern by gently stating, "I don't mean to upset you, or make you angry, but I hate to see you like this. How can I help?" Another approach is to say, "I'm concerned about you, your health and your safety. I'm here to help."

Always seek professional help and *never* try to tackle it on your own. Accept that it's beyond you and your control, and get counseling. Here are some strategies you may think about using while you're waiting for your appointment with the college's therapist:

- *Take lots of walks and be in nature.* Being outside can remove yourself from whatever problems you may be experiencing.

- *Spend time with friends.* Describe to your friends what you're experiencing. They may not be able to help you but at least let them know. Spending time with them can help you take your mind off things.

- *Tell your professors about the problem in a calm way.* You may need to talk to your professors if your depression is getting in the way of your work. You shouldn't go into detail—unless you are close to the professor— but let them know that you're experiencing some very difficult emotions and that you're talking to the school counselor. If you're late turning in work, tell the professor you can provide her with a referral from.

Suicidal Thoughts, Actions, or Other Self-Harming Behaviors

According to the Suicide Prevention Network, suicide is the third leading cause of death for those between the ages of 10 and 24 and the second leading cause of death for American college students (Kochanek, Murphy, Anderson, and Scott). According to a 2006 American College Health Association report, more than 40 percent of college students have felt so depressed they could not function. The 2007 tragic shootings at Virginia Tech have even more so highlighted undetected and untreated issues of mental health.

If you suspect your roommate may be having suicidal thoughts, here are some warning signs to help you determine if his or her life is in danger. If your roommate:

- Talks about death, dying, or any specific way she or he may die, even if it's in a joking way

- Has suffered or experienced a recent loss—death of family member or close friend, divorce of parents, terminal illness of someone close to him or her, job, financial security, religious faith, interest in activities

- Shows signs of depression—see symptoms above

- Displays noticeable change in personality—normally cheerful to sad and withdrawn, normally calm to irritable and nervous, normally organized to indecisive and sloppy, sudden mood change from sad to happy and energetic

- Displays different sleep patterns—waking earlier than usual, sleeping more than usual, unable to sleep

- Displays different eating habits—loss of appetite, increased appetite

- Talks about feeling worthless, helpless, guilty, useless, not having self-esteem, not being of any use to anyone, having no hope for the future, and says things like "The world would be better without me"

If you suspect your roommate may be planning to harm him or herself or may try to commit suicide, or if you are thinking of hurting yourself, call the National Suicide Prevention Lifeline at 1-800-273-TALK (8255) or the National Hopeline Network at 1-800-SUICIDE (784-2433).

Be especially concerned if you know this person has attempted suicide in the past. According to the American Foundation for Suicide Prevention, between 20-50 percent of people who commit suicide have had a previous attempt. Here are some vital skills and actions you need to practice if you have any suspicions that your roommate may be suicidal:

Take the threat seriously. If your roommate, or someone else you know, shows signs of depression and is contemplating or talking about suicide. Ask if he or she has a plan, weapon, or pills. Ask if he or she has taken any pills. Do not try to talk him or her out of it. Instead, let him or her know you care and are there to listen. Avoid saying, "But you have so much to live for," or "Everything will be fine." Don't just jump to a conclusion. Let him or her have the space he or she needs to talk.

Help the individual seek help, even if he or she does not think it is needed. You may have to show persistence. If he or she is unable to, offer to call a suicide hotline or call campus security or the university's suicide crisis hotline if applicable. If your roommate has already harmed him or herself, call 911 and then notify the front desk immediately.

Do not leave him or her alone. If you have to leave before help arrives or he or she gets immediate help, have someone else stay. If he or she appears drugged or is speaking in an incomprehensible way, call 911 and notify the front desk immediately.

Listen. Take the initiative to ask him or her what he or she is planning, but do not attempt to argue or convince him or her there is an alternative. Rather, let the person know that you care and understand and are listening. This is not the time to judge or criticize.

Remove any weapons or drug. Accompany him or her to the nearest emergency room if there is no one else there. It is all right to contact the RD so you have additional support. The RD will make the decision to contact parents.

Continue to support your friend. Encourage him or her to continue therapy and take medications.

Eating Disorders

Eating disorders affect people of all ages, but they are especially prominent in high school and college students. According to a 2011 study on eating disorders, "In the United States, 20 million women and 10 million men suffer from a clinically significant eating disorder at some time in their life, including anorexia nervosa, bulimia nervosa, binge eating disorder, or EDNOS."

They are a serious health concern that can result in chronic health problems and even death. Young people who suffer from eating disorders have creative ways of concealing them and are often in denial and refuse to seek treatment. It is possible for a roommate to hide an eating disorder from you, especially if you do not take meals together. You cannot solve or take responsibility for an eating disorder that belongs to someone else.

Eating disorders are not caused by any one factor but rather a combination of emotional, biological, interpersonal, and social factors. It is also likely that these disorders are a manifestation of a desperate need to establish some control and are triggered by stress. The transition to college, pressure to get good grades, and adjustment of living independently are stressful for students without eating disorders and can be triggers for those with them. The infamous "freshman 15," which represents weight gain upon entering college, only adds to the pressure for college students to lose weight.

Living with a roommate with an eating disorder cannot only disrupt your life and studies, but draw you into her obsession with food and body image issues. Eating disorders do not have to do with food, but are rather about gaining control over body image and pressure to comply with societal norms. While you cannot solve or take responsibility for her problems, you can become educated, aware, and offer help if you find yourself living with a roommate suffering from anorexia or bulimia. Here are some warning signs to look for:

Anorexia nervosa - Self-starvation and extreme weight loss

- Not eating or eating small quantities of food, weighing beforehand

- Fixation/obsession with food or rituals around preparing and eating food

- Constantly weighing himself or herself

- Distorted body image

- Wearing baggy clothes to hide weight loss

- Social withdrawal

- Excessive exercise

- Depression

- Fear of gaining weight

Physical signs of anorexia include dry, flaky skin, thinning hair, and cracked or broken nails. Women with anorexia often stop menstruating.

Bulimia nervosa or bulimia - Cycle of binge eating and self-induced elimination of food

- Eating large amounts of food in short periods of time followed by self-induced vomiting

- Misuse of laxatives, enemas, diuretics, or other medications

- Fasting

- Eating in secret

- Hiding food

- Out-of-control eating

- Noticeable feelings of loneliness and inadequacy

- Distorted body image

Physical signs may include discolored teeth, bad breath, swollen glands, staining or deterioration of tooth enamel, broken blood vessels around the eyes, fatigue, and stomach pain. Women with bulimia often stop menstruating.

Binge-eating disorder - uncontrollable, excessive eating, followed by feelings of shame and guilt. Those with binge-eating disorder do not purge their food. However, many who have bulimia also have binge-eating disorder and are overweight or obese. They feel like they have no control over their behavior and feel shame and remorse after eating.

- Eating in secret

- Hiding food

- Eating when stressed or overwhelmed

- Unable to control amount of food

- Constantly trying different diets

If you do not deem the situation to be an emergency (passing out, losing significant amount of weight, signs of depression, or self-harm), you can approach your roommate directly or seek assistance from university counseling on how to sensitively broach the topic. You can also educate yourself on eating disorders through pamphlets or seminars offered through student health or the counseling center.

If you directly address the issue with your roommate, pick a time when no one else is around to prevent interruption. Avoid making comments about her body or appearance. Do not "police" her food intake. People with eating disorders have a skewed body image and complex relationship with food.

Start with some positive attributes about your roommate, then focus on your concern, and state the behavior you have noticed that initially raised concern. Then state the outcome you would like to see. Use "I" statements when appropriate. Do not be disappointed if the first conversation does not go as planned. You may have to start the same conversations more than once so she hears your ongoing message of concern and offer to help. An example is:

Positive comment:

"You and I get along so well. I'm lucky to have you as a roommate."

State your concern:

"I'm concerned about the amount of weight you've lost the past few weeks."

"I'm worried about how sick you are."

Noticeable behavior:

"I've noticed you take your meals back to the room. We miss you at our table."

Desired outcome:

"I'd like to help you get treatment."

"I'll be happy to find out what kind of counseling is available for you."

"The university has a support group and crisis hotline. I have the number here for you to call."

You cannot or do not want to try to take control of behavior. You also do not want to tell her "things will get better," or to "snap out of it." Both are unrealistic. If either of you become upset or defensive during your conversation, it will only set things back for her. Take a break and suggest you talk later:

"Maybe we can talk about this tomorrow. I didn't mean to upset you. I just want to help in any way I can."

Meanwhile, Back at the Dorm . . .

There will be times when you notice that other people in the dorm are having issues while other people don't (perhaps not even their own roommates). This could be because you're more intuitive or observant than they. This does make it a little more difficult because while you're usually fairly familiar with your dorm-mates, it can be similar to the relationships you had with your peers in high school: friendly but distant. In high school, you may have noticed some depressed people or people with eating disorders and never felt close enough to say anything. Well, now is the time. College should be about expanding your moral sphere and becoming more selfless, although our highly individualistic culture in America might not promote it. In other words: If you see someone in your dorm suffering, do something. Don't just stand there and watch the car crash.

The best thing to do if you're not very close to them is to talk to their roommates. Ask them if they've noticed any issues and if they've talked to them about it. If not, suggest them having a conversation along the lines of what we've already covered in this chapter. This way, you know that while you can never take on a person's actions, you didn't just stand by and let it get worse. ∎

Anxiety Disorder

According to the National Mental Health Association, "College students are becoming the newest face of anxiety disorders," but only half of all Americans struggling with the condition seek treatment.

Just as some people have "depressive personalities," some people are naturally more nervous than others. Although this is often joked about in television and media, especially with chronic worriers such as Woody Allen, it's not always a laughing matter. Severe anxiety can be debilitating and even lead to depression. There is often a two-way relationship with the two, where anxiety overwhelms a person and causes them shut down emotionally (depressed), and this depressive state begins to create stress —and thus anxiety — in the person once more.

This isn't to say that if you feel stressed that it's "abnormal." It's true that every adult experiences various levels of stress at one time or another. It is a part of daily life and helps us solve problems and get through challenging situations. Levels of stress can be heightened at college where finals, new relationships, peer pressure, career choices, the availability of alcohol and drugs, and adjusting to independent living can trigger anxiety.

Unfortunately, since stress is rather common in our increasingly fast-paced world, most individuals who suffer from anxiety-related disorders believe they can control them, so they may go untreated.

The most common types of anxiety disorders are:

- Generalized anxiety disorder

- Panic disorder

- Obsessive-compulsive disorder

- Social anxiety disorder

- Post-traumatic stress disorder

Generalized anxiety disorder (GAD) is defined as having unrealistic, excessive worries about everyday things, expecting the worst, and feeling powerless to control these feelings. Symptoms may include irritability, difficulty sleeping or fatigue, difficulty concentrating, and muscle tension—some of which can occur daily. For college students suffering from GAD, there is much to worry about: grades, making new friends, safety, homesickness, and pressure to assimilate.

Panic disorder is defined by having recurrent and unexpected panic attacks. Symptoms of a panic attack may include heart palpitations, chest pain, smothering feeling, need to escape, disconnect from surroundings, sweating, trembling, and fear of dying or losing control. For college students suffering from panic disorders, moving about on a crowded campus, living in a cramped dorm room, or feeling stressed over exams or finals can trigger the symptoms. If your roommate is experiencing a panic attack, try to get him or her to breathe slowly and deeply as quick breathing only exacerbates the problem. See if you can get her away from the situation that may have brought on the attack, such as a going on a walk or moving to some place to take her mind off what is happening. You never want to suggest she drink alcohol or take a tranquilizer as they can have an opposite effect and make the situation even worse.

Obsessive-compulsive disorder (OCD) is defined by obsessive thoughts and actions that can control and disrupt a person's daily life and ability to form friendships and relationships. Symptoms may include complex, ritualistic behaviors and routines, such as repeated checking, counting, hand washing, and overall feelings of worry. People suffering from OCD may realize their behavior is out of the ordinary, but are unable to control it. Living with a roommate with OCD can be frustrating and difficult to understand for the other person and may impede on his or her comfort level in the dorm room. Most people experiencing OCD will need specialized therapy and perhaps controlled medication to overcome the disorder, as it is not likely to disappear on its own.

Social anxiety disorder (SAD) prevents the development of relationships and participation in social and professional activities in which other people are involved, such as parties, public speaking, and meetings. Symptoms may include heart palpitations, blushing, trembling, stammering, and light-headedness. For college students who suffer from SAD, being called on in class or being in a social situation in which they do not know anyone can trigger the symptoms. As in OCD, there is specialized therapy available for those who suffer from SAD.

Post-traumatic stress disorder (PTSD) affects people who may have experienced or witnessed a traumatic event, such as a serious accident, natural disaster, war experiences, sudden death of a loved one, or violent personal assault. Most people eventually recover from these types of trauma, but PTSD can also cause depression, other anxiety disorders, and withdrawal from family, friends and society. College students who are victims of rape or physical assault may suffer from PTSD.

If you are living with a roommate who suffers from one or more of these disorders, it is going to be frustrating and may affect your interaction with her and, possibly, your daily life. College is a stressful time, so you do not want to jump to conclusions if your roommate talks about feeling stressed or displays some behaviors associated with these disorders, but continuous, noticeable symptoms are indicators that your roommate needs help.

Healthy Encouragement and Counseling Services

You and your parents have worked hard to get to this point. Depending on your choice of colleges, someone is shelling out between $10,000 and $40,000 a year for you to get an education. Higher education is a major investment not only in money for personal growth and your future. Are you willing to spend a portion of this short time playing nurse or caretaker to a roommate with a mental illness or substance abuse problem? Or are you solely focused on getting good grades, preparing for graduation, or seeking professional employment?

You may be someone who has little time or concern for a roommate who binges, abuses drugs, or is constantly depressed. This does not mean you are a bad person. For some students who come from a family of modest means, spending more time in college beyond four years is simply not an option. If you will have student loans upon graduating, take that responsibility seriously, you will be focused on getting good grades and securing a job post-graduation. For those students who do not have the time to invest in bettering their roommate, they should seek the help of the RD when their roommate's chronic mental health problem starts to negatively affect their daily life and ability to study and stay focused on academics.

For those who want to try to help, know that denial, shame, and embarrassment are some of the reasons people suffering from mental health issues do not seek help. Educating yourself on the perceived problem before trying to initiate an empathetic conversation will provide informed guidelines and boundaries. Offer gentle, non-judgmental support and listen to what they have to say, even though it may be a new experience to you or provides a level of discomfort.

You can encourage them to seek help, but do not be surprised if your offer is met with continued resistance. People can have preconceived reasons why they should not seek counseling or why it would not work for them. They may think counselors have their own problems or that is too expensive. They may think counselors are only interested in prescribing medication or delving into childhood experiences that have little to do with the present. People can also be critical of counseling because they consider therapists "strangers" whom they cannot trust, rather than viewing them as trained professionals. Also, to most people, there is a level of discomfort in talking about a behavior of which they are ashamed. They would have to first admit there is a problem, and many cannot even get to that first step.

You can help debunk the myths surrounding counseling by assuring your roommate that it is confidential and helping her find out if the cost is covered by insurance. However, like any mental health issue your roommate may be experiencing, you cannot hold his or her hand all of the time. He or she has to be willing to address the problem, acknowledge it and eventually seek help on his or her own.

Meanwhile, Back at the Dorm . . .

You will find that a good portion of people in your dorms are struggling with some issue of some kind. Maybe they're overly religious and push their views on other people. Maybe they're depressed. Maybe they party too much and have issues with substance abuse. It's life: We're all born with battles we'll have to fight within ourselves. This will be especially prevalent when you're living in close contact with a large number of people.

This is why you should focus on developing your social life outside of the dorm. While it's tempting to just make friends in the dorms (they're literally right there, right?), it's highly recommended that you make an effort in your classes. These people will be a great resource: you can study with them, go off-campus for homework sessions, discuss areas of study you may pursue, and more. The best part about these friendships is they're developed from shared ideas and values, not just sheer proximity ▪.

CASE STUDY: TAKING THE DORM BY STORM

Melody Wolf
University of Florida

I chose to live in a dorm my first year of college because I wanted to get the full college experience. Living on campus allowed me to fully immerse myself in the college environment. Nearly everything was about a 15-minute walk, which made it easier to go to the gym or library without wasting gas money. My particular dorm was Beaty West. My roommates and I were on the 12th floor, which was not a huge problem since we had an elevator. When the fire alarms went off, however, the trek up and down the 12 flights was quite a hassle. (If anyone is interested in living in a dorm, it is important to find out the school's guidelines. For our university, your place in line for picking your dorm is determined by when you submitted your application.)

My freshman year, I roomed with three other girls. There were two of us to each room, and we all shared the bathroom and kitchen. Most things in the apartment were fair game, but there were a couple of items in which we had to set boundaries. Food was the main thing. Two out of the four of us were on a strict food budget, only receiving a limited amount of money for each month. Each person had her own shelf in the fridge and pantry. I always made sure to ask before I used something that wasn't mine.

All of my roommates seemed to get along the first semester . . . until what we call the "donut fiasco." After winter break, one of my roommates (let's call her roommate #1) decided to eat a donut on the kitchen table without asking, and that donut happened to be roommate #2's. What roommate #1 failed to know is that these were special birthday donuts ordered specifically by roommate #2's best friend. They both had very similar personalities, which turned a bad situation into a horrible one. From the donut fiasco on, there was no turning back. Roommate #2 ended up leaving us after the dorm contract was extinguished, and I will always go back to the donut scenario for her reasoning.

I would have to say one of my fondest memories of living on campus was walking to the gym with my roommates. Before college, I had never been much of a gym person. Being on campus, access to the gym was painless and free. My roommates motivated me to become more active, and I always looked forward to our late-night dates on the elliptical. We didn't always see eye-to-eye, but the few things we could always agree on were the gym, Subway, and Grey's Anatomy.

I wouldn't say my roommates were the best at conflict resolution. Whenever someone would get mad, that person would usually bicker to the other roommates instead of confronting the person head on. There was always some level of awkwardness, but fights were minimal. The most important thing to avoiding conflict is to limit your time together. Going from living full-time with family to living full-time with friends might seem like a party at first, but young adults are also messier, stay up later, and have little respect for boundaries.

Overall, I don't regret living in a dorm. I liked everything being in walking distance, including the dining hall (the Freshman 15 is real). I highly recommend experiencing dorm life to any incoming freshman. If anything, it will give you an appreciation of how nice being back in a full-sized bed is when you go home.

Chapter 7

Off-Campus Housing, Growing Up, and Greener Pastures

The dorms can, admittedly, be pretty silly. In a lot of ways, it may feel like you're at a summer camp: your meals are cooked for you, you may even have bunk beds, every night feels like a constant slumber party, and you're growing and changing almost every single day. You even have RDs that function as your chaperones and "daily activities" such as going to class and school events. It may seem like babying, but it definitely serves the purpose of making you feel like you have a support network to land on when things feel like they're out of control. There's no way you would be able to transition from living with your parents all your life to living in an apartment by yourself.

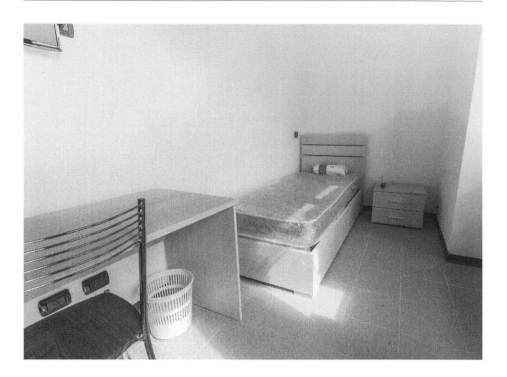

But at what point does it become coddling? At what point is it, perhaps, too expensive to keep living in the dorms? Living in the dorms can be at least twice, if not three times, as expensive as living off-campus. And you can't live at summer camp forever. And if you do, be prepared to get some pretty weird looks when you're still making lanyards at age 75. At some point, the babying has to stop. Meals have to stop being made for you. RDs can't keep intervening whenever there's a problem. You don't need constant interaction with your peers; you need to become self-sustaining.

Now, people have different preferences. If you feel like staying in the dorms because it will allow you to devote 100 percent of your energy to your studies, then by all means, *please*, do that!

But maybe you're just a little bit interested in your college town. Does the downtown have an allure that speaks to you? Are you interested in interning for a company there? Volunteering with the homeless shelters, schools, community organizations, or churches? The realities of adulthood are waiting for you, and you may find invaluable resources in the city that could lead to a rich and promising future. Perhaps you live in a vibrant city with lots to do: comedy clubs, festivals, museums, conventions, plays, galleries, open mics—you name it. Or perhaps your college is in a lovely small town, and you think you and a few good friends might be able to rent a beautiful historic home. Maybe you want a taste of something just a little more than the university bubble.

Depending on your college's restrictions, you *may be required to live on-campus for a certain amount of time.* Usually, this is either your first year or maybe two. This is probably for the best: don't just jump on it right away. Give yourself the time you need to adjust, and then look at your options.

What green pastures await you? This chapter details what to expect and how to get to your new off-campus home.

The Pros and Cons of Off-Campus Housing

To make it simple for you, here's a list of the pros and cons of off-campus housing. You'll want to consider these carefully, as once you leave campus housing, it can be really competitive to get back in.

Off-campus Housing	On-campus Housing
Pros	**Pros**
Independence You can learn how to cook, solve problems on your own, get your own room and space, do more independent activities, have people over when you want, get a car, etc.	*Support Nearby* You'll be surrounded by student resources. Students will always be nearby, and so will your RDs, health centers, libraries, classes, student store, and more. Basically, you'll never feel stranded and you'll have continual support.
New Experiences Studies show that novel experiences make for a happy life. The same old thing can get incredibly boring, especially if the campus is small and sleepy.	*Academics* Students tend to perform at a much higher rate when they're living on campus. The reason is not exactly clear, though it probably has something to do with how convenient everything is. You're also constantly reminded that you're *in school* and should be doing *school-related things* by living at it!
New Friends and Freedom Probably the best part about living off campus is the freedom. If you don't like your living situation, you can simply move and find a new place. You'll also get a chance to befriend and possibly live with people in town. Or, maybe you've found friends in your major and found a house together. Without the dining hall, you'll get a chance to learn how to cook in your own kitchen. The world's your oyster!	*Convenience* You wake up at 7:30 a.m. for your 8:30 a.m. class. Enough said.
Cheaper Off-campus housing is usually significantly cheaper.	*Community* Living with other students can create a strong sense of community that you might not get when you live off campus. Spontaneous outings and school events are much more accessible when you live on campus.

Off-campus Housing	On-campus Housing
Cons	**Cons**
Inconvenience Depending on how far out you live, living off campus can be a major inconvenience. You have to make sure to bring *everything* you need to school, and that you have *everything* before you leave.	*Over-dependence* Yes, there is such a thing as over-dependence. As you're growing into adulthood, you don't want to be coddled by other people.
Disconnection/Loneliness You may feel similar to how you did when you first moved in: lonely and without support. While it's not as big of a transition, it's definitely still a lot to get used to.	*No Privacy* Living in the city or town can offer you more privacy compared to living on campus. On campus, you'll constantly run into people you know, which can be a good or bad thing, depending on your perspective.

Can We Still Be Friends?

So you decide to move on from the roommate that was given to you in the college dorms. You found some friends in one of your favorite classes, you're moving into a new apartment, and you can't *wait to move away from her because she drives you nuts!* Maybe she knows this deep down, and there's a residual silence as you talk about your housing plans for next year.

One of the reasons it is best to be up front and honest with your roommate when either of you has moved on is that you may get that person to think about the possibility that he or she had issues. With a few exceptions, most people do not like confrontation, and we all avoid it or put it off if possible, making excuses or just dreading the possibility of hurting someone's feelings.

But if you lie about the reasons you requested a move and assume that out of 25,000 students or fewer you will never run into him, think again. One student told me she could not bring herself to tell her ex-roommate she requested a move because of her poor hygiene. So she lied and said she was transferring to another college. Sure enough, she ran into her on campus and lied again, telling her that she changed her mind at the last minute.

There will and have been many instances in which former roommates not only remain friends, but look back on whatever the conflict was and either laugh, scratch their heads or feel embarrassed that it ever got to the point of wanting to separate. You are only 18 when you start college and will have a whole different perspective on what is important by the time graduation roles around or if graduate school is on the horizon. Arguing about leaving wet towels on the floor seems childish when you are studying for the LSAT, and your future may depend on how well you test.

Finding a Place and New Housemates

During your first two years of college, don't be surprised if you're feeling angsty. You'll feel a lot of pressure to just "figure it out" and decide on your major. When you're an adult, it's easy to laugh it off because you realize how silly it is. But it certainly is stressful at the time, and the best thing to do is experiment. Your first two years are essentially spent "shopping around," and, funny enough, you usually take a class on the last semester of your second year that you absolutely love and this will decide your major for you.

You'll meet some fantastic people in college in a myriad of wonderful ways. If you do decide to move off-campus, make the move with people you really trust. If these people are your dorm-mates, so be it. If they're fellow students in your philosophy class, go for it. Make sure, though, that you really trust them. If they're your friends and they have issues, then stay friends. Don't become housemates.

Sometimes, it's best to look for single rooms. My last year of college, I really lucked out. I found a single room in a beautiful purple Victorian house close to the independent cinema where I worked. There were three other people who lived there: an older gentleman, a vibrant and energetic freelance artist in her 50s, and a fellow student from my school who was majoring in psychology. My room was beautiful, I saved money to decorate it, and it felt like the first thing that was truly mine in my adult years. I came and went when I pleased; I cooked fantastic meals, rode my bike around town, and had my friends from all around come visit. It was a truly wonderful and exciting time.

The people, place, and timing are crucial factors. Make sure your first gut instinct when meeting the people you'll be living with is: "Yes!" They say, in life, if it's not a "heck yes!"—it's a "heck no." If the location is convenient and the house is pleasant, then this is a "heck yes!" If it's far off, highly priced, dingy, poorly managed, or dirty this is a definite "hello no." Timing means that you feel ready to move off-campus. If you don't feel ready, don't feel pressured just because all your friends are moving off-campus: if it's not your time, it's not your time.

Lastly, you have all your adulthood to be an adult. Right now, you're a *young adult.* You have some license to experiment, to stumble, make mistakes, and lots and lots of room to grow. Don't rush into it, and make sure you always bring a sense of joy into whatever it is you do, whatever living situation you decide on. Otherwise, what's the point?

Conclusion

This book has hopefully provided helpful information on selecting campus housing and being prepared to live in peace with a stranger you will call "roommate." These pages also provide guidance on how to live, or decide not to live, with a problem roommate, from recognizing conflict and attempting to resolve it on your own to seeking help. The stories, interviews, and summaries from college and post-college roommates provide even more insight into what goes on behind closed doors in dorms around the country. Even if you breeze through your four years in college without one argument, this book will guide you through residential housing so that you are prepared to concentrate on academics, rather than the noisy, obnoxious, disrespectful, self-centered individual you may find yourself sharing a room with.

Keep this book next to your bed, in plain sight, so when the first conflict arises, you will not only have a reference guide on what to do next, but send a message to your roommate that perhaps she or he should flip through the pages as well.

Bibliography

"When Girls Will Be Boys," *New York Times Magazine*, March 2008, pp. 32-37.

"Colleges and Universities with Nondiscrimination Policies That Include Gender Identity/Expression." Campus Pride. Web. 26 Jan. 2017.

Antinozzi. G., Axelrod, A., *The Complete Idiot's Guide to Campus Safety*, Alpha Books, Published by the Penguin Group, New York, NY, 2008.

Bernstein, M. and Y. Kaufmann, creators, *How to Survive Your Freshman Year*, Hundreds of Heads Books, LLC, Atlanta, GA, 2008.

Brinkman, R., and R. Kirschner, *Dealing With People You Can't Stand*, McGraw-Hill, Inc., New York, NY, 2002.

Coburn Levin, K., and M. Lawrence Treeger, *Letting Go: A Parents' Guide to Understanding the College Years*, Fourth edition, HarperCollins, New York, NY, 2003.

Cohen, H., *The Naked Roommate*, Sourcebooks, Inc., Naperville, IL, 2005.

Deutsch, M., P. Coleman, and E. Marcus, eds. *The Handbook of Conflict Resolution*, Jossey-Bass, San Francisco, CA, 2006.

Dobkin, R. and Sippy, S., *The College Woman's Handbook*, Workman Publishing Company, Inc., New York, NY, 1995.

Farrar, R. and Worthington, J., The Ultimate College Survival Guide Fourth Edition (Ultimate College Survival Guide), Peterson's Educational Center, **www.petersons.com**.

Harrison, Jr., H., *1001 Things Every College Student Needs to Know*, Thomas Nelson, Nashville, TN, 2008.

Hitti, M., *College Students May Hide Self-Harm*, WebMD Medical News, June 6, 2006, **www.webmd.com**.

Janson, J., The Real Freshman Handbook: A Totally Honest Guide to Life on Campus, Houghton Mifflin Company, New York, NY, 2002.

Johnston, J. and M. Shanley, *Survival Secrets of College Students,* Barron's Educational Series, Inc., Hauppauge, NY, 2007.

Lang, S., "Self-Injury Is Prevalent Among College Students, but Few Seek Medical Help, Study by Cornell and Princeton Researchers Finds," Cornell University, Chronicle Online, June 5, 2006, **www.news .cornell.edu.**

Leinwand, D., "College drug use, binge drinking rise," USA TODAY, The Associated Press, 2007.

Malone, M., *The Everything College Survival Book: From Social Life to Study Skills—All You Need to Fit Right In* (Everything: School and Careers), Adams Media, Avon, MA, 1997, 2005.

Piven, J., D. Borgenicht, J. Worick, and B. Brown, *Worst-Case Scenario Survival Handbook: College*, Chronicle Books, LLC, San Francisco, CA, 2004.

Podlasiak, M., *Rules for Roommates*, Writers Club Press, New York, NY, 2000.

Scott, G. Graham, *A Survival Guide for Working with Humans*, AMACON, New York, NY, 2004.

Scott, G. Graham, *Disagreements, Disputes, and All-Out War*, AMACON, New York, NY, 2008.

Wade, T. D., Keski-Rahkonen A., & Hudson J. (2011). Epidemiology of eating disorders. In M. Tsuang and M. Tohen (Eds.), *Textbook in Psychiatric Epidemiology (3rd ed.)* (pp. 343-360). New York: Wiley.

Glossary

Anxiety A mental disorder characterized by unhealthy levels of stress and arousal in daily life.

Bigotry Intolerance towards people from different backgrounds, belief, or value systems.

Bipolar Disorder A manic-depressive disorder characterized by feelings of euphoria followed by an intense depression.

Conflict Resolution Methods of communication and navigating conflict with the end goal of resolving differences and coming to a compromised solution to the problem.

Depression A mental disorder characterized by persistent feelings of sadness and hopelessness. Other characteristics include lack of motivation, suicidal thoughts, and cynicism.

Dorm-mates People who live in other rooms in your residential hall. The quantity of dorm-mates depends on the relative size of the school and the hall itself.

Eating Disorder Any disorder that involves an unhealthy relationship with eating that has negative effects on one's physical and/or mental health. This includes but is not limited to bulimia, anorexia, and more. Usually arises from other mental health issues such as high levels of stress or depression.

Homophobia Prejudice against people of a different sexuality than oneself.

Living Learning Communities A dorm hall that's allotted to students who need a quiet living area to focus on their studies. Quiet hours may be earlier in LLCs.

Off-campus housing Off-campus housing can be provided by the university or sought out by the individual student. Students usually chose to pursue off-campus housing options once they are more settled in their academics, usually one or two years after beginning college.

On-campus housing On-campus housing options may be dorm-halls that have limited appliances or apartment buildings. On-campus apartments usually include a kitchen and a living room, where dorm-halls do not.

Personality Spectrum A spectrum of different personalities that may include but are not limited to: neatniks, slobs, kleptomaniacs, gossips, whiners, aggressors, and more.

Post-traumatic Stress Disorder (PTSD) A disorder characterized by high levels of stress arising from a past traumatic event.

Residential advisor The person in charge of facilitating peace within a residential hall. These are usually students who are very good at navigating conflicts and sought out a job on campus to help with their tuition expenses.

Substance Abuse Dependence or unhealthy relationship with substances.

Suicidal Ideation Ideas spawning from a desire to kill oneself. Anyone who discusses ideas or plans to kill him or herself is in need of immediate help, and any such statements should be reported to 911 immediately.

Additional Resources

Mental Health and Substance Abuse

Suicide Hotline: 1-800-784-2433, open 24 hours a day, seven days a week

National Hopeline Network: 1-800-442-4673, **www.hopeline.com**

American Foundation for Suicide Prevention: **www.afsp.org**

Al-Anon/Alateen — Friends and Families of Alcoholics: **www.al-ateen.org**

National Mental Health Information Center: **www.mentalhealth.org**

National Institute of Mental Health: **www.nimh.org**

HealthyPlace.com: **www.healthyplace.com** (online depression resource and community)

Campus Blues: **www.campusblues.com**

National Association of Anorexia and Associated Disorders: **www.anad.org**

National Eating Disorders Association: **www.NationalEatingDisorders.org**

www.collegedrinkingprevention.gov

Poison Control Center: **1-800-222-1222**

Safety and Health

National Sexual Assault Hotline: 1-800-656-HOPE

College Safety Guide: to download, visit **www.collegesafe.com**

Allergy and Asthma Network/Mothers of Asthmatics, Inc. (AAN/MA) **www.aanma.org**

Gay, Lesbian, Bisexual, and Transgender

Gay and Lesbian Hotline: 1-888-843-4564, **www.glnh.org**

Parents, Families and Friends of Gays and Lesbians: **www.pflag.org**

National Coalition for Gay, Lesbian, Bisexual, and Transgender Youth: **www.outproud.org**

Lambda Legal and Educational Defense Fund: **www.lambdalegal.net**

American Civil Liberties Union: **www.aclu.org**

Off-Campus Housing

www.campus1housing.com (comprehensive site, searchable by college, for off-campus housing)

www.campusroommates.com, which includes a comprehensive listing of ads that are specific to a college or university, such as:

www.craigslist.com (free site to find and post cheap stuff, roommates, services)

www.roommates.com (searchable roommate database by state)

www.campusroommates.com (searchable database by state, college, city. Ads can be posted also

Index

About the Author

Melanie Falconer grew up in the vibrant and ever-so-wonderful Bay Area, California. She could be found at coffee shops reading, doodling, eating old lasagna, or performing on stage at her local community theater. If she's being candidly honest, she deplored high school, which made her believe that humans were meant to live like cattle, being shuttled from one thing to the next. At her college, U.C. Santa Cruz, she discovered that she could seize her education and life by the reins. She explored her interests in writing, Spanish, theater, and linguistics, graduating with a B.A. in Language Studies.

Her freelance projects include writing for blogs, helping students edit their essays, creating educational content for high school students to study for their AP exams, and writing young adult nonfiction such as *College Study Hacks: 101 Ways to Study Easier and Faster* and the book you have in your hands.